INAT*

IMAGES OF

SERBIA &
THE KOSOVO
CONFLICT

*REGARDLESS OF THE CONSEQUENCES

ABOUT THE AUTHOR

Scott Taylor, a former soldier, is the editor and publisher of *Esprit de Corps**, an Ottawa-based magazine celebrated for its unflinching scrutiny of the Canadian military. Research for this book was compiled first-hand from inside Yugoslavia and Kosovo during the NATO air campaign and its aftermath. Taylor appears regularly in the Canadian media as a military analyst, and is the recipient of the **1996 Quill Award** for outstanding work in the field of Canadian communications. That same year, he won the **Alexander MacKenzie Award** for journalistic excellence.

Taylor has been a contributor to *Maclean's*, the *Globe and Mail*, *The Financial Post*, *Media Magazine* and *Reader's Digest*. In addition, the majority of on-site reporting which appears in this book was produced on freelance assignment for the *Ottawa Citizen* and the *Toronto Sun*.

OTHER WORKS BY SCOTT TAYLOR

♦ ***Tarnished Brass: Crime and Corruption in the Canadian Military***
  (with Brian Nolan), 1996 (reprinted 1997)
♦ ***Tested Mettle: Canada's Peacekeepers at War***
  (with Brian Nolan), 1998
♦ ***Canada at War and Peace: A Millennium of Military Heritage***
  (editor-in-chief), 1999

* *Esprit de Corps* magazine is a monthly publication focusing on the news and history of the Canadian military. A 12-issue subscription costs $29.95. For additional information, contact 1-800-361-2791 (in Canada) or visit the *Esprit de Corps* website at www.espritdecorps.on.ca.

INAT*

IMAGES OF
SERBIA &
THE KOSOVO
CONFLICT

*REGARDLESS OF THE CONSEQUENCES

"There is no race which has shown a more
heroic desire for freedom than the Serbs, or
achieved it with less aid from others –
or at more sacrifice to itself."

TEMPERLY, BRITISH HISTORIAN

Canadian Cataloguing in Publication Data

Taylor, Scott, 1960 -
INAT: images of Serbia & the Kosovo conflict

Includes index.

ISBN 1-8958996-10-X

1. Kosovo (Serbia) – History – Civil War, 1998 – Participation, Foreign. 2. North Atlantic Treaty Organization – Yugoslavia – Serbia. I. Title.
DR1316.T39 2000   949.7103   C00-900218-9

Printed and bound in Canada

Esprit de Corps Books
1066 Somerset St. West, Suite 204
Ottawa, Ontario
K1Y 4T3
1-800-361-2791

From outside Canada
Tel: (613) 725-5060 / Fax: (613) 725-1019

INAT*

CONTENTS

Acknowledgements ~ **6**

Dedication ~ **7**

About this book ~ **8**

Maps ~ **9**

Chapter One: The Untold Story ~ **11**

Chapter Two: History Repeated ~ **21**

Chapter Three: First Strikes ~ **33**

Chapter Four: Into the Fray ~ **47**

Chapter Five: Surrealism and Suffering ~ **59**

Chapter Six: Disturbing the 'Peace' ~ **75**

Chapter Seven: Revenge and Retreat ~ **93**

Chapter Eight: Counting the Cost ~ **117**

Chapter Nine: Resetting the Stage ~ **143**

Chronology of Events ~ **149**

Index ~ **153**

ACKNOWLEDGEMENTS

The author wishes to acknowledge the contributions of those individuals whose talent and dedication made this project possible. First and foremost, recognition is due to Bora Dragasevich and his wife Draga. Without their belief and tireless efforts, *INAT: Images of Serbia and the Kosovo Conflict* would never have been written.

Special thanks go to Ljiljana Milojevic Borovcanin who arranged my media accreditation and helped me gain access to government sources in the Federal Republic of Yugoslavia.

While in Serbia, the research and filing of reports was ably expedited by the combined family efforts of Vlada, Zlatan and Radmila Kopric. On the homefront, Bruce Garvey deserves credit for editing and promoting the (almost) daily war reports which first appeared in the *Ottawa Citizen* and form the genesis for INAT. The last-minute edit by Penelope Body smoothed out the bumps and she was a pleasure to work with.

As usual, the production staff at *Esprit de Corps*, Cathy Hingley and Julie Simoneau, did a superb job of bringing this project to fruition. Their efforts are greatly appreciated.

Brian Nolan and Peter Worthington have been role models and mentors over the years. Their patience, guidance and friendship have helped *Esprit de Corps* to survive and have made projects like *INAT* possible.

A special thank you is due also to Miriam, Fred, Mary, Raymond and the Kirkness family for their collective support and financial assistance.

Dedicated to Katherine
for her understanding and courage.

ABOUT THIS BOOK

This work consists primarily of eyewitness observations and firsthand interviews collected during the Kosovo conflict and its bitter aftermath. It is not meant to be a comprehensive historical overview of the war. Rather, it is a personal account of events as seen from inside Serbia.

As such, the journal portion has been deliberately limited to information available to the author, in Serbia, at the time.

Throughout the war, thousands of western journalists spent months reporting on the air campaign from refugee camps in Macedonia. The stories they wrote of the Albanian Kosovars' plight were disseminated around the world. However, as every one of those reporters knew, they were only presenting one side of a complex situation.

INAT is the story of one correspondent's experiences on the other side of the battle line.

PHOTOGRAPHY

Unless otherwise credited, all photos appearing in this book were taken by the author.
Cover photo: The Yugoslav Army retreats from Kosovo.
Back cover photo: Funeral of four-year old Dijana Pavlovic.

ABOUT THE TITLE

Inat is a Serbian noun which does not directly translate into English, but roughly means "regardless of the consequences." Far from being just a simple word, *inat* is best described as a spirit which is embodied in the psyche of the Serbian people.

Over the past six centuries, *inat* has played a significant role in compelling the tiny Serb nation to resist the Ottoman Empire, challenge the Austro-Hungarian Empire and refuse to capitulate to the Nazi-German invaders. In every one of these David vs. Goliath struggles, the Serbian people have endured horrible suffering without losing their collective will to resist.

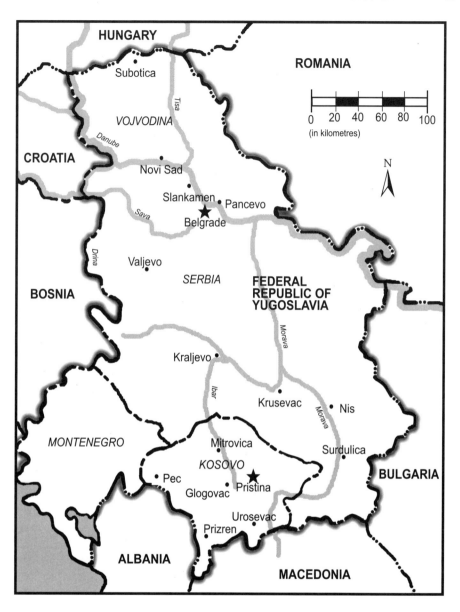

SERBIA AND KOSOVO, 1999: *The map shows the major cities in the Federal Republic of Yugoslavia which the author visited or reported on during the NATO air campaign and its aftermath.*

THE BALKANS 1999: *Since April 1992, Canadian peacekeepers have been continuously deployed to the former Yugoslavia. The war they witnessed often bears little resemblance to the one portrayed in the media.* **OPPOSITE:** *One major event that went unreported was the September 1993 four-day Battle of the Medak Pocket in which Canadians killed Croatian troops.* (PHOTO COURTESY MIKE O'BRIEN)

1 - THE UNTOLD STORY

Belgrade, May 27, 1999 (Wednesday) At 8:30P.M. the air raid sirens began to wail, anti-aircraft (AAA) cannons on the city's perimeter opened up, and streams of tracer-fire arced skyward. Less than a minute later a massive explosion erupted in the Belgrade suburb of Zemun, creating billowing clouds of black smoke. Following the blast, the entire city was plunged into darkness – the NATO airstrike had once again successfully targeted the Yugoslavian capital's power grid. The "all clear" siren did not sound until the following morning and bombs pounded Belgrade at least twice more during that interval.

From my candlelit room on the top floor of the landmark hotel, Moskva, I provided an eyewitness account of the attacks via telephone to a Toronto radio station. Undoubtedly, the poor phone connection and background thumping of AAA cannons added a measure of drama to the short broadcast.

Following my update on the situation inside Belgrade, the host thanked me, then asked: "On a personal note, just why are you there?"

Admittedly, it is uncommon for journalists to report from "inside the enemy camp" and, with Canada taking an active role in the NATO airstrikes, that is what my presence in Yugoslavia would have to be considered. The short answer was that I was one of the very few journalists fortunate enough to obtain an official entry visa into Serbia from the Yugoslav authorities. One would like to believe that every reporter in Canada would jump at such an opportunity – regardless of the risk – and I know that a long list of mainstream media representatives had, in fact, applied for such access. However, given my background (a soldier who created a magazine focused solely on the activities of the Canadian military), my position was somewhat unique. Since the very same soldiers, sailors and airmen who constitute *Esprit de Corps'* readership were mounting the offensive operations against Yugoslavia, many journalists questioned whether my reports from inside Serbia would alienate my regular readers. Given the input and feedback *Esprit de Corps* had received from peacekeepers prior to the Kosovo conflict, such an occurence seemed unlikely.

Since they were first deployed into the region in 1992, the majority of Canada's service personnel have served on at least one peacekeeping tour in the Balkans. Very few of them wholeheartedly embraced the concept of NATO becoming embroiled in a bitter civil war as one of the belligerents. Those with firsthand experience in the former Yugoslavia recognized that the complexity of the situation made it impossible to single out and assign guilt to any one faction. The Serbs, Croats and Muslims were all equally implicated in terror campaigns against each other's civilian populace (and in some cases against their own). As peacekeepers, it was often difficult for Canada's troops to maintain the necessary measure of objectivity in dealing with the various warring factions. On some notable occasions, Canadian soldiers did become engaged in firefights, either to defend themselves or to protect unarmed citizens. However, the concept of embracing any one of these combatants as an ally was unthinkable – it would amount to an insult to the soldiers' sense of propriety and professionalism.

Nevertheless, in February 1999, President Bill Clinton and the United States State Department did just that by launching the collective might of the NATO Alliance towards an inexorable martial showdown with Yugoslavia over the disputed territory of Kosovo.

That such an unprecedented offensive action by NATO could generate so much popular support throughout North America and Western Europe was a direct result of what can only be described as the media's demonization of the Serbs. Since the first armed clashes in 1991 heralded the breakup of the former Yugoslavia, the Serbs had been portrayed in the American press as "the heavies." Virtually overnight, the breakaway republic of Croatia and the Muslim-dominated independent Bosnian government had quickly and effectively won the global propaganda war. For television audiences thousands of miles away who had no personal stake in the Balkan conflict, the entire Yugoslavian civil war was dumbed down to a bad guy (Serbs) vs. good guy (Croats and Muslims) scenario. While this simplistic approach made it easy for the U.S. State Department to formulate policies, it in no way reflected the complex reality of the situation.

Canadian peacekeepers were frequently called upon to protect Serbian civilians from victimization and, in some cases, to record atrocities perpetrated by the Croats or Muslims. Far from the western media's portrayal of the Serbian militias as that of a conquering juggernaut, most Serb soldiers – particularly in the Canadian Areas of Operation (AOR) – were actually poorly trained, badly-equipped amateurs.

From 1992 to 1995, I made a total of six trips into Croatia and Bosnia to report on the experiences of Canada's peacekeepers. What became readily apparent was that nightly newscasts back home did not depict the same war-torn Yugoslavia being patrolled by our soldiers.

For instance, on September 9, 1993, the Croatian forces unleashed a massive bombardment on a Serbian-held enclave known as the Medak Pocket. This region, designated a United Nations Protected Area, was occupied by a Canadian infantry battalion. Following the artillery fire, the Croats launched a pincer-like attack that effectively eliminated the Serbian defenders from the ridgelines. Along the valley floor, Croat tank columns quickly captured four Serb-held villages. Over the next three days, in an effort to fulfil their "protection" mandate, Canadian soldiers from the Second Battalion Princess Patricia's Canadian Light Infantry (2PPCLI) engaged the Croatian special forces units in a number of firefights. Official reports later stated that some 35 Croats were killed during the skirmishes, while four Canadians were wounded by artillery fire. Through this stoic display of determined resistance, the commander of 2PPCLI, Lieutenant Colonel Jim Calvin, eventually convinced the Croatian commander to withdraw his forces. Before pulling out, the Croats massacred all of the remaining Serb inhabitants. Ordered not to interfere by U.N. Headquarters in Zagreb, the Canadians were forced to stand by as unwilling, impotent witnesses to the carnage. The only recourse possible for 2PPCLI was to catalogue the evidence they had collected, and to seek official U.N. indictments against the Croat commanders as war criminals. Despite the overwhelming evidence, the Croatian government issued a brief, blanket denial, and the whole issue was quickly dropped. The general who had planned and executed the Croatian attack was, in fact, an Albanian Kosovar named Agim Ceku.

The 1993 action at the Medak Pocket garnered only fleeting coverage on CNN and incredibly, given the magnitude of our soldiers' actions, went completely unpublicized by the Canadian defence department. In fact, the Canadian public did not even *learn* of the engagement until three years later, when *Ottawa Citizen* reporter David Pugliese broke the story on October 7, 1996. (It wasn't until May 1998 that Lieutenant Colonel Jim Calvin finally briefed Parliament – complete with photographic evidence of the massacre.)

For the soldiers who took part in the harrowing Medak operation – Canada's largest ground battle since the Korean War – the lack of public recognition was disturbing. Warrant Officer Matt Stopford was awarded a Mention in Despatches for his courage under fire and for maintaining his position during the first days of the Croatian bombardment. His forward observation post was just metres from the Croat front lines. Thus, during the last night before the withdrawal, Stopford had been an eyewitness to drunken Croat special forces troops – one of whom was parading around with bloodied panties on his head – raping, looting and killing Serbs with impunity. The restrictive U.N. Rules of Engagement prevented Stopford from doing anything but reporting the atrocities to a higher headquarters.

Upon returning to Canada, Stopford was amazed at the ignorance of the average citizen. "People would hear that you'd just got back from Yugo, and they'd say 'aren't those Serbs bastards?' as if they knew all about the Balkans," said Stopford. "When you'd start to explain to them how we watched the Serbs get butchered by the Croats, you could see their eyes glaze over. Nobody really wanted to give that much thought to the complexity of the situation in Yugoslavia," Stopford continued. "For us, it was like coming home from the Second World War and telling people we'd fought *for* the Germans. Rather than try to explain things, it was easier just to let it go."

On August 3, 1995, in the same sector that Lieutenant-Colonel Jim Calvin's 2PPCLI had resisted the Medak Pocket incursion, the Croats launched *Operation Storm*. This time, the Canadian peacekeepers did not resist. Rather than endanger their own lives, the men of the Royal 22nd Regiment (Vandoos) surrendered their weapons and observation posts to the advancing Croats. Once again, under the direction of General Agim Ceku, the Croatian Army unleashed a devastating artillery bombardment. This time, however, it was German mercenaries in Croatian uniform who spearheaded the attack, and NATO fighter jets that provided them with tactical airstrikes.

The Serb defenders of this region (known as the Krajina) didn't have a chance – tactically or strategically. The moment the artillery bombardment began, Serb civilians – aware of the massacre conducted by Ceku's troops in the Medak – began to flee into Bosnia *en masse*. Their soldiers were right behind them.

Nearly 250,000 Serbs were thus 'ethnically cleansed' from the Krajina in advance of the Croat onslaught. Those who chose to remain – or were too tardy in their flight – paid the price. As Ceku's men swept through the Krajina, all evidence of Serb habitation was systematically destroyed. Civilians were executed; livestock and pets slaughtered; houses burned; and wells poisoned. When thousands of fleeing Serbs sought refuge in the Krajina capital of Knin, General Ceku's artillery gunners deliberately shelled the city. According to U.N. reports, over 500 civilians were killed or wounded in the bombardment – at a time when Knin was devoid of military targets. In other words, the shelling was an intentional act of terror against unarmed civilians, a war crime.

Two senior Canadian officials serving with the U.N. were present in Knin at the time of the attack, Major General Allain Forand and Colonel Andrew Leslie. Both men submitted detailed complaints to the U.N. War Crimes Tribunal in an effort to indict not only the commanders (including Ceku, who was responsible for the artillery), but also Croatian President Franjo Tudjman. General Forand and Colonel Leslie alleged that only Tudjman himself could have authorized the massive Krajina cleansing and the terror bombardments.

Even though Canadian peacekeepers had been captured and detained during the attack, there was almost no domestic media coverage of the forced displacement of 250,000 Serbs, not to mention the accompanying slaughter. For the Canadian military, the shameful surrender by the Vandoos was an embarrassment that senior commanders understandably did not wish to have publicized.

Since the U.S. had covertly aided the Croats in *Operation Storm* (through the provision of arms, training, advisors, satellite intelligence and airpower), the massive Serbian tragedy went virtually unreported in North America.

In contrast, just three weeks earlier, the eyes of the world (via the cameras of CNN) had been focused upon Serbian aggression and atrocities as Serbs overran the long-suffering Muslim enclave of Srebrenica. For many Canadian soldiers, the increasingly biased media coverage was difficult to accept. "It's not a case of believing in a *justifiable revenge* philosophy such as 'two wrongs make a right' or 'an eye for an eye,'" said Howard Michitsch, a former infantry major who served as a military observer in the Krajina. "But, if the press only tells one side of the story, it distorts the equation, and precludes any rational comprehension. We step onto a slippery slope when people start drafting far-reaching policies and solutions based on such incomplete information."

Even on the front lines, Canadian soldiers have learned that all is not as it might first appear. During the seven years they have been monitoring conflicts throughout the former Yugoslavia, the Canadians have witnessed innumerable cases of various factions *staging* incidents in order to blame their opponents. Invariably, it has been the Muslims who have proven to be the most ruthless and relentless employers of this tactic – and the most successful at garnering a sympathetic response.

On February 5, 1994, when a 120mm mortar shell exploded in Sarajevo's Muslim market killing 68 and wounding 197, international film crews were on hand within minutes to record and broadcast the horrific images. Immediately, the wheels were set in motion for NATO to begin punitive airstrikes against Serbian artillery positions. President Bill Clinton and Secretary of State Madeleine Albright based their hard line on "the perception" of Serbian culpability. Using this incident as a catalyst, the U.S. State Department negotiated a Croat-Muslim coalition and began launching airstrikes against the Serbs. Totally ignored in the ensuing international fracas was a French lieutenant's detailed report, which concluded the 120-mm shell had been fired from "inside the Muslim lines."

In his 1997 book, *The Sharp End: A Canadian Soldier's Story*, author Jim Davis detailed an incident where he and his comrades were handing out candies to Muslim schoolchildren in a Sarajevo suburb. The playground came under sudden mortar attack, shells cleaving a lethal wake through the cluster of tiny bodies. Davis and his men were later informed by U.N. officials that the shots had been fired by Muslim gunners hoping to create an incident that would be blamed on the Serbs.

During the two-year siege of Sarajevo, United Nations observers noted that the majority of cease-fire agreements were violated by the Muslims themselves. A favorite tactic was to 'provoke' the Serbs into retaliating by shelling them first.

This proved particularly effective after the February 1994 "heavy-weapons-free zone" was proclaimed by the U.N. in response to the market massacre. With U.S. airpower overhead to enforce the Serbian withdrawal, the Muslims could (and did) fire with impunity.

On the evening of July 3, 1994, I witnessed a Bosnian-Muslim detachment fire a recoilless cannon into their own town of Visoko. The resulting explosion was the impetus for yet another broken cease-fire, as the Muslims then "avenged" the attack by engaging the Serbian trench lines with machine-gun fire. I was visiting a detachment of the Lord Strathcona's Horse (LdSH), a Canadian Armoured Regiment manning a nearby observation post. They immediately reported the Muslim duplicity which had sparked the firefight. Sergeant Tom Hoppe was in command of the small LdSH unit, and, caught up in the middle of the fray, his section and I spent over four hours pinned down under sustained fire.

While manning the same post ten days later, Hoppe's men were once again the targets of hostile fire. As they tried to withdraw from their exposed position, Muslims attacked them from point-blank range. In the ensuing combat, Trooper Jason Skilliter fired a 30-round burst into two Muslim militiamen, killing them both. After discharging smoke grenades from their two armoured personnel carriers (APCs), Sergeant Hoppe's men were able to successfully fight their way off the contested ridgeline without casualties.

By the next morning, the Muslims had removed all traces of the firefight. The two men whom Skilliter had killed were buried unceremoniously in a village 17 kilometres away and, to prevent any "revenge" attacks, the local unit was rotated away from the Canadian position. Hoppe and Skilliter were quietly decorated for their bravery under fire, but the Canadian government never officially acknowledged the killing of two Muslims – and the Muslims never complained.

"Had Serbs been killed that night, Hoppe's guys probably would have got the U.S. Congressional Medal of Honour pinned on by Madeleine Albright herself," said Tom Martineau, a retired Warrant Officer formerly with the Lord Strathcona's Horse. "Instead, because it didn't fit the picture they wanted to sell to the public, [the Canadian] government treated the whole thing like it was some sort of dirty little secret."

With the major media outlets paying only scant and sporadic attention to our troops in Yugoslavia, the Canadian government could easily keep such information from the public. That, in turn, made it far easier for our Foreign Affairs ministry to conform to the U.S. State Department's Balkan agenda without fear of domestic backlash.

Of course, they couldn't keep the truth from soldiers who had seen things in the Balkans for themselves. Thus, when the international sabre-rattling over Kosovo began in the fall of 1998, climaxing with the first NATO airstrikes against Yugoslavia on March 24, 1999, the most vocal opposition to our military intervention came from Canada's veteran peacekeepers.

As a matter of professional honour, those still in uniform refrained from criticizing policies which emanated from our democratically elected Parliament. However, a host of retired senior officers took the government to task over the prospect of committing Canadians to punitive strikes against the Serbian people. The most prominent critic was former United Nations Protection Force (U.N.PROFOR) Commander Major General Lewis MacKenzie. (The retired MacKenzie has been steadfast in his attempts to counter the media's demonization of the Serbs.)

Joining MacKenzie was Colonel Don Ethell, Canada's most experienced peacekeeper. Shortly after the commencement of hostilities, Ethell led a delegation to Ottawa to express his outrage over the NATO bombings. (Over the previous six years, I had crossed paths with Colonel Ethell on several occasions, publicly debating military issues with him. Although we had disagreed in the past, I applauded his courage in speaking out against a government policy he found reprehensible.)

In April, as the NATO air campaign stalled and talk of a ground war grew, two former members of the army unexpectedly visited my Ottawa office. They said that, given their experiences in Bosnia, an order to fight against the Serbs would place them in a moral dilemma tougher than any they had encountered in their careers.

They had seen firsthand the covert U.S. involvement in building up the Muslim and Croat forces. At the same time, as members of the U.N., the Americans were trying to stabilize and demilitarize the region. Their experiences left them leery of the current U.S. propaganda on Kosovo, and they were unwilling to buy into the wholesale dehumanizing of the Serbian people.

◆　◆　◆　◆　◆　◆　◆　◆

They were not alone. Medak Pocket veteran Matt Stopford had begun to openly question NATO's support of the Kosovo Liberation Army (KLA) as far back as February 1999.

As ultimatums were bringing the Alliance ever closer to war with Yugoslavia, a new player quietly entered the scene. In U.S. newspapers it was announced as a positive development that a top Croatian general had resigned from his post to take over command of the KLA guerrilla forces. Agim Ceku was going home – as a hero and Canada's ally.

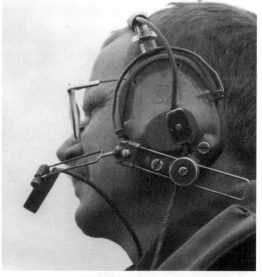

ABOVE LEFT: Based on his experiences in Sarajevo, Major General Lewis MacKenzie has maintained that all factions, not just the Serbs, are responsible for the atrocities in Yugoslavia. (DND)

ABOVE RIGHT: Warrant Officer Matt Stopford witnessed Croatian troops massacre innocent Serbs in the Medak Pocket. Those Croats were commanded by Albanian Kosovar General Agim Ceku.

RIGHT: Ceku took over command of the KLA in February 1999. Top Canadian officers wanted him indicted for war crimes committed in Croatia in 1993 and 1995. (JNA)

ABOVE: *Serbian refugees from the Krajina region try to peddle their belongings for food after they were forced from their homes by the Croats in 1995.* (PHOTO BY AUTHOR)

OPPOSITE PAGE: *A similar exodus occurred three centuries earlier following the 1690 Battle of Skopje. Once the Ottoman forces had destroyed the combined Serbian Austro-Hungarian army, many Serb Kosovars fled the vengeful wrath of the returning Turks. Led by their patriarch, 35,000 Serb families fled Kosovo in what has since been labelled the Great Migration.* (ILLUSTRATION COURTESY SERBIAN NATIONAL SHIELD SOCIETY OF CANADA)

2 - HISTORY REPEATED

Outsiders cannot visit the Balkans without being inundated by history lessons. Each ethnic faction can recite a detailed account of their forefathers' exploits; each tale contradicts another told by a traditional neighbour-cum-enemy.

It is difficult for North Americans to understand just how deep-rooted such sentiments are. Nor can we fully understand the still passionate reactions to events which occurred over 600 years ago. During the NATO air attacks against Kosovo, errant bombs damaged several historical, religious landmarks. Throughout Serbia, citizens were outraged at the wanton disregard shown by NATO pilots for such sacred structures.

"In this regard, we Serbs are very naïve," said Zlatan Kopric, a Belgrade-based computer specialist. "We expect Americans to respect something which they cannot even fathom." As a resident of a 300-year-old heritage building, Kopric explained, "My *toilet* has more history than the United States of America."

In analyzing the recent, tragic developments in Kosovo, it is impossible to divorce the present from the past. It is imperative to first understand Serbian nationalism and ethnic pride. To do so, one must examine the history of the region.

From the twelfth through to the fourteenth century, the Serbs created a remarkable medieval empire. Ironically, it is the collapse, rather than the nadir, of this glorious era that has taken on mythical proportions. On the Kosovo *polje* [the field of blackbirds] in 1389, in an attempt to turn back an Ottoman invasion, Prince Lazar Hrebeljanovic fielded a tiny Serbian army. Against a battle-seasoned phalanx of approximately 45,000 Turkish *janissaries*, the Serbs pitted a mere 20,000 untested volunteers. Realizing the odds of victory were slight, Lazar exhorted his men with the phrase, "It is better to die in battle than to live in shame."

The Turks summarily vanquished the outnumbered Serbs. However legend has it that every one of his soldiers heeded Prince Lazar's final dictum. Rather than submit to the Turkish invaders, they held their ground and died where they stood. The Kosovo *polje* ran red with Serbian blood and "no surrender" became a cornerstone of Serb culture.

A subplot to the vivid stories that surround the Battle of Kosovo has is that the heroic Serb defenders were defeated by the Turks solely as a result of a fellow Serb's treachery.

While only loosely based on fact, the label of traitor has been firmly attached to the legacy of Prince Lazar's son-in-law, Vuk Brankovic. By pointing a finger at the treasonous culprit, the Serbs have been able to perpetuate the belief that only through unity will Serbia prevail.

While Prince Lazar's epic 1389 battle is commemorated as the event heralding Turkish occupation, it was not until 1459 that the Ottoman conquest of Serbia was complete. During that 70-year interval, the fields of Kosovo *polje* would twice more echo with the sounds of battle. Thousands of Serb warriors chose to follow their martyr's lead and sacrifice themselves rather than live in shame under Turkish rule. (At the second Battle of Kosovo in 1448, the story goes, Vuk Brankovic's son Djurad betrayed his countrymen.)

The legends of martial selflessness and defeat through disunity continued to grow. As the Ottomans solidified their control over the Balkans in the late fifteenth century, many vanquished Serbs chose to abandon their homesteads and flee north. In the wake of the Serbian exodus, the first major wave of Christian Albanians poured into Kosovo.

For the next two centuries, the remaining Serbs and ethnic Albanians lived side-by-side in Kosovo, in relative harmony, under the overall control of the Turkish governors. However, as an increasing number of Albanians converted to the Muslim faith to avoid paying the Ottoman's "Christian tax," a major rift developed. The Serbs, encouraged by their Orthodox priests and the example of Prince

Lazar, refused to reject their religion. As a result, the Albanians enjoyed relative prosperity, while the Serbs became increasingly impoverished. Predictably, when the Austro-Hungarians challenged the Turkish Empire in 1690, they found the Serbs a willing ally.

Unfortunately for the Serbs, the Sultan's armies prevailed once again, delivering a devastating defeat to the Austro-Hungarians at the Battle of Skopje. Fearing Turkish reprisals, 35,000 Serb Kosovar families fled with the retreating army. In 1737, the occupying Turks conducted a second major "ethnic cleansing" of Kosovo, forcing thousands of Serbs from their homesteads.

These displaced Serbs were resettled throughout the Austro-Hungarian Empire, largely to create a buffer zone which would prevent further Turkish expansion. Large Serb enclaves were created in Bosnia and the Krajina during this period, known as the Great Migration. To retain their sense of identity and culture, the widely scattered Serbs turned increasingly to their folklore – the legends of Lazar and the battlefields of Kosovo.

In 1878, the Russians were able to capitalize on the Serbian desire to reclaim Kosovo. During the Russo-Ottoman war, the Tsar enlisted the Serbs as allies. Under the command of Serbian Prince Milan Obrenevic, a combined Serb-Montenegrin force invaded Kosovo and defeated the Turkish defenders. In the eyes of the Serbs, Prince Lazar had finally been avenged. Obrenevic's soldiers immediately began the task of reclaiming the province. Their first action was the expulsion of about 30,000 Muslim Kosovars followed by the destruction of their mosques.

Unfortunately for the Serbian victors, their spoils of war were short-lived. At the Congress of Berlin, the Russians negotiated a peace deal with the Ottoman Empire. Under the terms of that agreement, Serbia and Montenegro were formally recognized as independent states. However, Kosovo would remain under Turkish control. Having to give up their re-captured province left the Serbs feeling betrayed by their Slavic protectors.

The Albanians who remained in Kosovo also resented the return of Ottoman control. They felt the Turks had failed to protect their interests and, under the leadership of the newly-constituted Prizren League, an armed Albanian nationalist uprising occurred. The Ottomans were able to crush the Prizren League's revolt, but the embers of the Albanian Kosovars' independence movement would continue to smolder.

In 1912, Serbia formed a military alliance with Greece, Montenegro and Bulgaria to oust Turkey from the Balkans. It proved to be a costly war. Nevertheless, in the end, the Serbs not only recaptured Kosovo, but, this time, their occupation of the disputed province was sanctioned by the international community. At the 1913 Conference of the Ambassadors in London, a stroke of the pen officially awarded Serbia her long-coveted prize.

Once again, the celebration proved to be short-lived. Less than one year later, Bosnian Serb Gavrilo Princip shot and killed Austrian Archduke Franz Ferdinand on the streets of Sarajevo. Within days, the Austro-Hungarians had declared war on Serbia, and Russia had begun to mobilize in support of their Slavic ally. After Germany declared solidarity with the Austrians, Britain and France upped the ante by pledging support to the Tsar. The world was at war.

From the north, tiny Serbia was invaded by the Austro-Hungarians, supported by Bulgarian and German forces. In Kosovo, Albanian *Kachak* guerrillas mobilized and supported the Ottoman Turks in their campaign against Serbia. Attacked from all sides by a superior force, the outcome was inevitable. Nevertheless, the Serbs fought valiantly against overwhelming odds. By October 1915, the Serb Army had been shattered, but they would not surrender. In an epic winter retreat, approximately 100,000 soldiers accompanied by thousands of refugees followed the Serbian royal family south across the Kosovo *polje*. After a torturous 60-day trek over the Montenegrin mountains into Albania, the battered Serb force was embarked by the French and British navies. Starvation and exposure had claimed 20,000 soldiers and 60,000 Serbian civilians. However, regrouped and re-equipped on the Island of Corfu, the Serbian Army returned to action – in Salonika – in October 1916. During the fall of 1918, this same Serbian force spearheaded the French and British offensive to push the Austrians and Turks out of the Balkans. By the time the armistice was signed, the Serbs had not only liberated their own country, but they had forced the Austro-Hungarians from Slovenia and Croatia as well.

At the postwar 1920 Treaty of Trianon, the appreciative French and British governments rewarded the Serbs by creating a single Yugoslav umbrella state in which Serbia would be the dominant republic.

Kosovo would once again be formally recognized as Serb territory. Although unified on the new world maps, the fledgling kingdom of Yugoslavia would remain internally divided by ethnic hatred and mistrust. The Croats, Muslims and

Macedonians all harboured a measure of resentment towards their Serbian over-seers. In Kosovo, the rapid pace of Serbian resettlement caused angst among the Albanian population. The new Serbian authorities shut down the former Otto-man schools, as well as Muslim Kosovar cultural facilities, and replaced them with their own. Violence became commonplace, and the Albanian nationalists re-emerged as the *Kachak* separatist movement.

When Hitler invaded Yugoslavia in 1941, it did not take him long to reignite age-old hatreds. The Yugoslav Army was quickly routed – the entire country was overrun in just three weeks – but the resistance movement took to the hills. The majority of partisans were Serbs, and they were divided into two distinct camps. Serbian nationalist Dragoljub Mihailovic led the Royalist Chetniks, while the Serb communist guerrillas followed Josip Broz Tito, a man of mixed Croat-Slovene heritage.

Hitler's Nazis had no trouble recruiting volunteers to fight the Serbs. Croatia was established as an independent state and declared its allegiance to Germany. The Croats raised an SS Division, *Ustasha*, that soon earned a well-deserved repu-tation for brutality and ruthlessness against the Serbs. Italian fascist dictator Benito Mussolini had occupied Albania earlier in the war, and he, too, quickly took ad-vantage of the splintered situation in Yugoslavia. He granted control of Kosovo to the Albanians and, in cooperation with the Germans, these Muslim Kosovars re-cruited their own SS Division, *Skenderberg*.

The main target of the *Skenderberg* were Serbs who had recently resettled in the province. Thousands of Serb civilians were killed; more than 70,000 fled their homes in Kosovo to seek refuge in Serbia. Later, as Marshal Josip Broz Tito's partisans gained the upper hand, the Germans were forced to pull out of Kosovo. Fearing a return to Serbian authority, the Albanians continued to resist in the hope that the province would become part of Albania.

Their efforts proved futile.

In the post-war reshaping of Europe, Tito was able to establish firm control over a complex structure known as the Federation of Yugoslav Republics. The new Yugoslavia consisted of six separate republics: Bosnia-Hercegovina, Croatia, Macedonia, Montenegro, Serbia and Slovenia. Serbia included two 'autonomous regions,' the Vojvodina and province of Kosovo. Scattered throughout all of these administrative zones were the numerous, and mutually distrustful, ethnic fac-tions.

Marshal Tito understood that the key to keeping the lid on the new nation was to dampen the divisive fires of nationalism. "A weak Serbia makes a strong Yugoslavia," was his oft-repeated motto.

The Albanian separatist movement in Kosovo experienced a resugence in 1953. After the Yugoslav president broke off relations with Soviet leader Joseph Stalin, the staunchly pro-Stalinist Albanian government began to support independence activists in Kosovo. Tito clamped down, severely curtailling the province's autonomy. Suppression only fanned the emotional flames. Throughout the 1960s, large-scale riots were commonplace as ethnic Albanians demanded a separate republic.

In response to the mounting pressure, Tito reinstated full autonomy to the province in 1974, authorizing the creation of a national bank, universities, administration and a supreme court. The Serb Kosovars feared the Albanian majority would misuse their newly-authorized powers. For their part, the ethnic Albanians felt cheated out of their quest for full independence. Rather than quell the unrest as Tito had hoped, the compromise generated a new round of separatist riots.

Following Tito's death in 1980, there was a resurgence of nationalism among all the ethnic factions. On April 24, 1987, the lid finally blew off the simmering pot of divisive patriotism. The individual responsible for this eruption was then-Deputy President of Serbia, Slobodan Milosevic, who had done so by invoking the long dormant spirit of Prince Lazar to inflame passions in Kosovo.

Milosevic had been dispatched to Kosovo *polje* to *quell* the growing dissent among Serb Kosovars. They had been complaining to the central Belgrade government that Albanian authorities were systematically harassing them. Milosevic's presence in Kosovo was intended as a show of concern on the part of the Serbian government. A large crowd of Serb Kosovars expected more. When they became unruly, the Kosovo police moved in with riot batons. At the height of the melée, Milosevic addressed the assembled Serbs: "Nobody shall beat you again! This is your country, these are your houses, your fields and gardens, your memories. You are not going to abandon your lands because life is hard, because injustice and humiliation oppress you. It has never been a characteristic of the Serbian and Montenegrin people to retreat in the face of obstacles, to demobilize when they should fight... Yugoslavia does not exist without Kosovo! Yugoslavia and Serbia are not going to give up Kosovo!"

TOP: By October 1915, the Serbian Army had been shattered by the combined forces of Austro-Hungary, Germany and Bulgaria. Rather than surrender, the remnants of the Serb military retreated south through Albania. Thousands of refugees fled with them. (IMPERIAL WAR MUSEUM)

ABOVE: When Hitler's armies occupied Yugoslavia in 1941, their primary military opposition was from Serbian partisans. Reprisal executions by the Nazis became commonplace on the streets of Belgrade. The corpse of a suspected partisan is left hanging from a lamp post in front of the Hotel Moskva as a warning sign to the resistance movement. (JEWISH MUSEUM, BELGRADE)

A former banker, Milosevic had been regarded as just another faceless communist party *apparatchik*. However, after the Kosovo *polje* address, "Slobo" became the focal point for a renewal of Serb nationalism. In 1989, riding the wave of new-found popularity, Milosevic was elected president of Serbia. To deliver his inauguration speech, he chose to return to Kosovo *polje*. This time, an estimated one million Serbians cheered on the 600th anniversary of Prince Lazar's legendary battle from the time-honoured fields. Three months earlier, Milosevic and the Serbian Assembly had amended their constitution to rescind Kosovo's autonomy.

The reaction from the Albanians was predictable. Forced underground, with their parliament disbanded, the separatist movement began to arm itself for a terrorist campaign. The fledgling Kosovo Liberation Army (KLA) took the place of its *Kachak* predecessor.

By 1990, the first armed clashes were taking place between the now Serbian Kosovar police and Albanian separatists.

Western Europe and the international media paid little attention to these internal developments. The situation in Kosovo was completely eclipsed by the fragmentation of Yugoslavia in June 1991. The split began with the proclamations of independence by Slovenia and Croatia (followed by Bosnia in April 1992). Four years of brutal civil war ensued, followed by ruthless campaigns to purify zones of control known as "ethnic cleansing." Serbia, while not directly involved in the conflict, supplied men and weapons to the Bosnian Serbs and the Krajina regions. Although the combined Serb forces achieved early successes, the imposition of international trade sanctions, coupled with the U.S. provision of military aid to the Croats and Muslims, reversed their fortunes. By the time the Dayton Peace Accord was enforced in 1996, the Serbs had suffered tremendous losses.

In addition to the estimated 20,000 soldiers killed, more than 750,000 Serbs had been cleansed from Croatia and Bosnia. Trade sanctions remained in place against the rump Republic of Yugoslavia, now comprised of only Serbia and Montenegro. The economy was in tatters.

During the 1996 municipal elections, the people had exercised their democratic right to send the Belgrade government a message. The opposition won an overwhelming majority over Milosevic's party at the ballot boxes. However, when these results were ignored, the electorate was outraged.

Hundreds of thousands of Serbs took to the streets night after night to protest the presidency of Slobodan Milosevic.

Milosevic's concerns over growing domestic unrest were compounded by steadily increasing Albanian terrorist activity in Kosovo. To cope with the flood of Serbian refugees displaced by the war, the Yugoslav government had initiated a resettlement program in Kosovo. Ethnic Albanians saw this as a deliberate ploy to alter the region's demographics, thereby precluding their eventual independence. The separatists stepped up their campaign of terror. Milosevic had responded by increasing both the number and capabilities of his security forces in Kosovo.

On November 29, 1997, a funeral was held in Drenica for an Albanian teacher who had been killed by Yugoslav police. When two masked, armed men appeared, the mourners began to chant U-C-K, the Albanian slogan for KLA. Soon the chant could be heard across the province.

As the KLA gained control of rural areas, Yugoslav police units were bolstered by elements of the Vojska Jugoslavije, the regular army and reservists. On March 5, 1998, a Serbian battle group surrounded Adem Jashari, the KLA commander, at his mountain outpost. Jashari and his followers refused to surrender and were killed. Jashari became a martyr, and the fighting intensified.

By July, the widening conflict drew the concern of the European community. Despite international pressure for a cease-fire, the Serb forces mounted a major offensive in August to reclaim the area previously seized by the KLA. Roughly 45 per cent of the province was under Albanian control and guerrillas were operating just five kilometres from Kosovo's capital, Pristina.

As Yugoslav troops regained the tactical initiative, the United Nations Security Council passed Resolution 1199. Both parties were to agree to an immediate cease-fire, and the Yugoslav security forces were to withdraw. Failure to comply with the directive would trigger "additional measures [being taken by the U.N.] to maintain or restore peace and stability."

There was always the likelihood of a Russian or Chinese veto, since NATO countries had been instrumental in pushing the Kosovo resolutions through the U.N. Security Council. However, NATO officials publicly declared they would ignore any veto. Their aircraft were poised to launch punitive airstrikes against the Serbs and, with or without U.N. approval, they intended to bomb.

Milosevic appeared to concede and, by October 27, 1998, his armoured forces were returning to their barracks. Part of the U.N. resolution called for the deployment of "unarmed international verifiers" to monitor the cease-fire in Kosovo. Throughout November, nearly 2000 observers arrived in the war-ravaged province to find that the firing had never really ceased. Since their setback at the hands of the Serbs in August, the KLA had been re-equipped and trained by international "advisors" in Albania.

As the Serb armour pulled back, the new, improved KLA renewed their guerrilla attacks on Serb police forces with a vengeance.

On the diplomatic front, things were also beginning to unravel. Milosevic had agreed to the concept of a U.N. Verification Force, but he balked at allowing Louise Arbour, the Canadian judge serving as the chief prosecutor for the U.N. War Crimes Tribunal, to conduct an investigation into alleged Serb atrocities.

For their part, the Albanian Kosovar delegation had split internally. Ibrahim Rugova, the pacifist delegate, was prepared to make several key concessions to the Serbs. From the outset, Rugova had been opposed to the use of KLA terrorism to achieve independence. Hashim Thaci, the KLA leader, was not so accommodating. Denouncing Rugova's conservative approach, and emboldened by his rising status within the NATO community, Thaci proclaimed the KLA to be the sole representative of the Albanian Kosovars. As Rugova appealed to the U.N. to deploy peacekeepers to Kosovo, Thaci ordered his men to resume the war.

On January 16, after months of scattered fighting during which it became increasingly apparent that the KLA was being furnished with sophisticated weaponry by NATO sources, the crisis came to a head. At the village of Racak, U.N. verifiers discovered 40 Albanian corpses and evidence of torture. Serbian officials claimed the dead were KLA terrorists, but their protests fell on deaf ears.

Although heavily embroiled in the Monica Lewinsky impeachment scandal, American President Bill Clinton took to the airwaves to express his outrage over the Racak incident. NATO reiterated that they were prepared to impose a military settlement if an agreement could not be reached between the Serbs and the KLA.

Both warring factions were instructed to send delegates to Rambouillet, France to hammer out an accord by February 19.

NATO instructed the Serbian government that failure to participate would result in airstrikes against Yugoslavia; the KLA was told that a lack of compliance would mean a suspension in provision of military aid. Even to the casual observer, it became evident that, despite claims of impartiality, NATO was clearly in the KLA camp.

As the peace talks got underway in Rambouillet, Serbian apprehension mounted. When negotiations stalled, U.S. Secretary of State Madeleine Albright met secretly with the Albanian delegation. She outlined three possible options: 1) they could refuse to sign the American draft proposal and thereby lose all NATO support; 2) they could sign the deal and, if the Serbs refused, NATO would bomb them into accepting the deal; and 3) both parties would agree to the conditions and NATO troops would enforce the agreement.

Under the terms of the Rambouillet Treaty, there would be no referendum on Kosovo independence for at least three years. For KLA delegate Hashim Thaci, such a delay was unacceptable.

The Serbs had a number of objections to the proposal, not the least of which was the plan calling for NATO troops to be allowed free access to Yugoslavian airspace and land routes. Ostensibly, this was simply to facilitate the establishment of a NATO peacekeeping force in Kosovo. The Serbs saw it as an occupation of their homeland. The guarantee of an eventual referendum on Kosovar independence was another thing they were not prepared to accept.

When the original deadline passed with neither side having signed, Albright once again approached the Albanians. She advised them that she now had a fourth option: If both sides refused to sign, NATO would withdraw the threat of airstrikes against Yugoslavia. On February 24 the Albanian delegates proposed a hasty compromise, suggesting a two-week delay, which would allow them time to consult with the residents of Kosovo.

Once again, heavy fighting erupted in the war-torn province. Serbian police forces were reinforced, and Yugoslav air defence units were reportedly deployed to strategic sites inside Kosovo.

On March 15, the Albanians announced they would agree to the Rambouillet terms. As a matter of courtesy, the Serbs were given one last opportunity to sign the accord. Since no new concessions were being offered, they refused. On March 18, at the Arc de Triomphe in Paris, the Albanian Kosovars signed sole approval of the peace deal.

Madeleine Albright's second option, the bombing of Belgrade, was cleared for take-off.

ABOVE: *Four Canadian CF-18s flew as part of the first wave of NATO bombers which struck targets throughout Yugoslavia on March 24, 1999.* (PHOTO COURTESY DND)

OPPOSITE PAGE: *Outraged by the attack, the Serbian people filled the streets in a spontaneous display of patriotism and defiance.* (PHOTO COURTESY RTS)

3 – FIRST STRIKES

Belgrade, March 24, 1999   Katarina Njegovan was heading home from the Belgrade university just after 8:30P.M. when she heard the startling news over the radio; NATO warplanes had just bombed Kosovo and southern Serbia. Driving along in her old Volkswagen Beetle, the 22-year-old philosophy student waited for the disc jockey to admit his news bulletin had been a hoax. By the time she parked in front of her house, the eerie sound of air raid sirens confirmed her worst fears. Belgrade was under attack.

Katarina's neighbours reacted by either running outside or watching from their windows, all the time shouting questions at each other and staring skyward. Nobody knew what to expect. The Njegovans decided against heading to an air raid shelter but, for safety's sake, they moved their bedding into the basement.

For 81-year-old Andjelka Kopric, the sound of the sirens brought back a flood of memories. Born in 1918, the final year of World War I, she had been raised on tales of the hardships and suffering the Serbs had endured during the four years of fighting. She was just 22 when Hitler's *Luftwaffe* appeared in the skies above Belgrade in 1941, spearheading the German invasion. Over the next four years, she witnessed the brutal atrocities committed by the occupying Nazi forces.

Andjelka did not intend to seek shelter from this latest threat in a damp bunker. Instead, she quietly set about making a list of survival necessities and preparing jars of preserves.

When Bojan Bugarcic learned of the first bomb attack, he was furious. As the senior foreign affairs advisor to President Slobodan Milosevic, Bugarcic had been one of the Yugoslav diplomatic negotiators in Rambouillet. Until the NATO-imposed deadline, he had been holding productive telephone discussions with his U.S. counterpart, Ambassador Richard Holbrooke. Since these talks were ongoing, the bombing came as a shock to Bugarcic.

The Yugoslav diplomat immediately telephoned Holbrooke in his Budapest hotel room. "Just what the hell do you think you're doing?" Bugarcic screamed. Before hanging up, Holbrooke reportedly replied, "This is not a take-it-or-leave-it situation. It's a take-it-or-we'll-make-you-take-it situation."

March 25, 1999   It didn't take the Serbs long to recover from their shock. Overnight, their initial fears were replaced by defiant outrage in the face of NATO's blatant aggression.

Political differences and internal dissent were set aside as spontaneous, massive demonstrations were held to reaffirm Serbian solidarity in defence of the fatherland. Almost immediately, Serbian communities around the world emulated what had begun in the central squares of Yugoslavian towns. Just prior to the NATO deadline, virtually every embassy official in the Yugoslav capital had packed up and headed for Budapest. In Belgrade, the mobs vented their frustration and anger on the abandoned embassy buildings.

In the Canadian cities of Toronto and Ottawa, Serbian community leaders organized the first of what would become nightly protests in front of U.S. consulates and embassies. In the wake of the initial air attack, all foreign journalists registered in Belgrade were rounded up by the military police and ordered out of the country. The reason given was logical enough – to prevent the dissemination of information that could be used by NATO for intelligence purposes. However, it would soon prove to be a costly error for the Serbs. NATO spokesman Jamie Shea became, by default, the primary source of war news.

Consequently, much of the information on what was transpiring in Yugoslavia, came not from Belgrade but from NATO headquarters in Brussels, Belgium.

Setting aside all journalistic ethics and common sense, the press corps attending Shea's daily briefings dutifully reported even the most jingoistic of claims. "We have a report," was all Shea needed to say, and the next news flash was on the wires.

March 27, 1999   The night after the western media were thrown out of Belgrade, the Serbian Air Defence scored a major victory. Over the hills south of Belgrade, their primitive, anti-aircraft cannons tracked and shot down a U.S. ultra-sophisticated F-117 Nighthawk Stealth fighter plane. Built at a cost of nearly $2 billion each, the top secret F-117 is billed as "invisible to radar," and "invulnerable to anti-aircraft rockets." Images of the wreckage were broadcast by jubilant Yugoslav television networks and Serbs were soon trumpeting the slogan, "Sorry Bill [Clinton], we didn't know it was invisible."

To counter this public relations setback, NATO tried to focus attention on the successful rescue of the Stealth's pilot. As an added distraction, Jamie Shea made the shocking announcement that Yugoslavs had emptied their jails of hardened criminals and sent them to fight in Kosovo. Widely reported, this story soon became 'fact.' Incredibly, no one questioned how this information had been obtained. As the tale made good copy, it went unchallenged.

March 29, 1999   From the breakdown of the Rambouillet talks to the onset of the NATO airstrikes, the moderate Albanian delegate, Ibrahim Rogova, had kept in touch with Slobodan Milosevic's regime. His longterm objective had always been an independent Kosovo, but he believed it should be achieved through peaceful means. As NATO bombs rained down on his province, and both the Serbian forces and the KLA stepped up their attacks, the Albanian leader remained in Kosovo determined to break the diplomatic impasse.

Hashim Thaci's KLA saw Rugova's continued entreaties to Milosevic as a traitorous act. Extremists declared Ibrahim Rugova an enemy. With this, the rift which had developed between Rugova's Kosovo Democratic League (LDK) and Thaci's KLA reached the breaking point.

At NATO headquarters Jamie Shea took a different approach. After proclaiming that Rugova was under "house arrest" in Kosovo, NATO released unconfirmed reports that Milosevic had executed the Albanian in rash retaliation for the NATO air raids. As word of this alleged murder spread around the world, images of Slobodan Milosevic and a very-much-alive Ibrahim Rugova were broadcast on Serbian television. Jamie Shea casually dismissed the images as a "pre-recorded trick." As far as NATO was concerned, Rugova was dead and Milosevic was responsible.

March 31, 1999   By the end of the first week of bombing it became apparent to NATO planners that their objectives had not been met. In fact, their concept of a *graduated response* air campaign was backfiring. Not only had they stirred the Serbs into collective defiance, they had also precipitated a mass exodus of refugees from Kosovo. Four days after the first bombs dropped, approximately 8000 Albanians had crossed the border to seek sanctuary in Macedonia. Seventy-two hours later, that trickle had become a flood, as more than 100,000 Kosovars fled their homes. The rationale that NATO had used to justify their intervention in Kosovo was that, by forcing the Serbs to capitulate, they could prevent a humanitarian crisis. Once they realized the bombing was creating an even greater crisis, NATO simply reversed their spin: Since a major human catastrophe was underway it was all the more imperative that the Alliance impose a solution.

The fatal flaw in the original NATO plan was the erroneous assumption that the 1995 airstrikes in Bosnia had been successful.

The purpose of those attacks had been to lift the 41-month siege of Sarajevo. The U.N. had imposed a 20-kilometre heavy-weapons-free zone around the embattled city and, beginning on August 30, 1995, NATO aircraft and U.S. cruise missiles had been employed to "convince" the Serbs to withdraw. During the next two weeks, the air operation, named *Deliberate Force*, reportedly destroyed much of the Bosnian-Serb military capability. Primary targets included ammunition and fuel depots, army barracks and vital transportation infrastructure. By September 13, Yugoslav President Milosevic, who was formally representing the Bosnian-Serb Republic at the peace talks, agreed to the U.N. terms. The next day, the Serbs pulled back their heavy calibre weapons.

The western press had trumpeted this as proof of the efficiency of the NATO airstrikes. The three-and-a-half-year Sarajevo stalemate was over. Those close to the situation knew better. One person who chose to publicly challenge the arm-chair-pundit's version was a Canadian – retired Major General Lewis MacKenzie. He wrote a letter to the editor of the *Toronto Star*, stating that the assertion the airstrikes lifted the Sarajevo siege was "child-like analysis." MacKenzie noted that,

48 hours prior to the bombing, Milosevic had offered to negotiate with the international community. Bosnia Serb leader Radovan Karadzic had also made a last minute overture to former U.S. President Jimmy Carter.

Once the bombs started to drop, Serbian officials immediately revoked their offers and adopted a more confrontational stance.

What had driven Karadzic and Milosevic back to the international bargaining table was not the punitive air attacks, but rather the success of a simultaneous Bosnian-Croatian ground offensive. In a single week, the Muslim-Croat forces had captured over 3900 square kilometres of territory and displaced an estimated 160,000 Serbian refugees. In agreeing to the peace terms, Karadzic admitted that the ground war had forced their capitulation. "We have sustained heavy losses and have lost several towns and territories that belonged to the indigenous Serbs for centuries," he said.

Nevertheless, NATO strategists chose to believe their own propaganda. With the Alliance's overall military objective limited to the vague concept of "downgrading Serb forces," the primary purpose of their graduated response had been to force Yugoslavia to accept the terms of the Rambouillet peace accord.

As it became clear that the airstrikes alone were not having the desired effect, NATO threatened to use ground forces. To make such an option, which would include the risk of heavy casualties, publicly palatable, it would be necessary to step up the propaganda war.

April 1, 1999   NATO spokesman Jamie Shea and his White House counterpart, Joe Lockhart, did not have to worry about winning over the all-too-willing press corps. There is perhaps no better example of jingoism than the news reports that followed the March 31 Serbian capture of three U.S. servicemen along the Kosovo-Macedonia border.

NATO aircraft had already launched seven straight days of airstrikes against Serbia. British and U.S. troops were pouring into Macedonia and Albania, threatening to begin ground assaults into Kosovo.

When Serbian soldiers engaged the three-man, U.S. reconnaissance patrol, the Americans returned fire. After a brief skirmish, the U.S. troops threw down their rifles and surrendered. It was war. Their air force was attacking the enemy, they were on the frontline, they fought back, and they were captured. It should have been nothing more than a minor embarrassment for U.S. martial pride. However,

NATO and the American media turned the incident into an example of Serbian "barbarism." The words used to describe the incident were not "capture" and "surrender" as soldiers would expect, but rather "kidnap" and "abduction." To stir American passions, President Clinton vowed to hold Milosevic "personally responsible," should any harm befall these brave boys.

In the days that followed, media coverage centred on the ever-increasing flood of humanity emerging from Kosovo. Tales of Serbian atrocities grew with the arrival of each new column of ethnic Albanians. International aid agencies estimated that Serb paramilitary forces had systematically executed 10,000 Kosovars since the air war began. Words such as "holocaust" and "genocide" were heard. In a bid for public support of a ground intervention, U.S. Secretary of State Madeleine Albright likened Slobodan Milosevic in 1999 to Adolf Hitler in 1938. In other words, the international community had a moral obligation to stop Milosevic's evil crusade before he could turn his Kosovo genocide into a Europe-wide holocaust.

The propaganda campaign had the desired effect. A poll conducted in Canada found that more than 76 per cent of respondents would support the decision to send in ground troops – with or without a prior peace agreement. In response, Major General MacKenzie wrote a column in the *Ottawa Citizen* pointing out that poll results are often determined by the way in which the question is phrased, and the knowledge of the people questioned. The public was upset by continuous images of fleeing Albanian refugees. The idea of sending in soldiers seemed simple: Not only did it sound good, but, for the majority of Canadians, it was also a remote commitment.

One veteran Canadian peacekeeper, assigned to the Kosovo task force, was amused by the poll result. "They all want *us* to go in there and fight, but I don't see any of *them* quitting their jobs to line-up at the recruiting centres," he said.

April 7, 1999   From the beginning, Canada had played an active role in the air campaign. Four of our CF-18 Hornets had been part of the initial NATO raid, and they had unleashed their recently-acquired smart bombs on Yugoslav targets. From that point on, Canadian pilots would account for 10 per cent of the strike sorties mounted by the NATO air armada. Just seven days into the war, Canada had "graduated" its own response, adding six additional CF-18s to the Wing already operating out of the airfield in Aviano, Italy. By the conclusion of hostilities, Canada had a total of 18 fighter aircraft over Kosovo.

TOP: *The wreckage of the passenger train at Grdelica. To bolster his claim that it had been an unfortunate accident, NATO spokesman Jamie Shea released video footage* **(INSET)** *showing the doomed train leaping into the pilot's sights. The video was later shown to be a fabrication.* (MAIN PHOTO COURTESY RTS, INSET COURTESY NATO)

RIGHT: *To eliminate "Serb propaganda," NATO planes attacked the Yugoslav television networks. For the first time in history, journalists became legitimate military targets.* (PHOTO COURTESY RTS)

ABOVE: *On April 14, 1999, NATO planes errantly targetted an Albanian refugee convoy on the Djakovica-Prizren road. In three separate airstrikes against the columns of wagons and tractors, 73 civilians were killed and 36 wounded. In the aftermath, NATO spokesman Jamie Shea suggested that Serbian warplanes "could have" been responsible for the attack. It was later confirmed that American jets had made "a regrettable error" in mistaking the tractors for tanks. (PHOTO COURTESY RTS)*

As our understrength air force struggled to meet their assigned objectives and maintain their logistic support (not the least of which was a chronic shortage of smart bombs), the army was also stretched to the limit. With a 1200-man peace-keeping force committed to Bosnia, and another 700 serving elsewhere around the globe, Canada had been hard-pressed to assemble an 800-man contingent for service in Kosovo. The original intention had been to deploy these troops as 'peace-keepers' to enforce the Rambouillet Accord. That mandate was replaced on April 7 by a far more ominous role. Following a top-level Liberal Party cabinet meeting, Defence Minister Art Eggleton announced during a media scrum that NATO was now considering the use of ground troops. In other words, if necessary, our peace-keepers would fight their way into Kosovo.

The U.S. military brass at the Pentagon were reportedly furious with Eggleton for this premature disclosure of the Alliance's plan. NATO hastily issued categori-cal denials, and Prime Minister Jean Chrétien issued a stern correction.

The Serbs were apparently inclined to believe Eggleton. In Kosovo, they closed the borders and began to lay fresh minefields.

April 9, 1999   After six years of continuous scandals and a string of attempted cover-ups, the Canadian military's public affairs branch had a well-earned repu-tation for being frugal with the truth. Journalists who covered the defence beat had long since learned to take the Department of National Defence's press confer-ences with a healthy degree of skepticism. However, from the outset of the Kosovo crisis, the media had been so unquestioningly compliant that even the public af-fairs officers, themselves, did not believe it could last.

For several consecutive days, DND had presented a string of successful airstrike reports detailing how many CF-18 aircraft had been launched from Aviano, and how many of these had engaged their intended targets. Luck had been on NATO's side, as the conditions (clear skies and moonlight) were ideal for air operations. However, bad weather over Kosovo had subsequently precluded our fighters from launching any missiles for two successive nights. Admitting to having launched 12 unsuccessful sorties in 48 hours would put a blemish on their heretofore stellar record, so DND decided to simply report how many aircraft had taken part in the air raids.

The Public Affairs Directorate realized that a sharp-eyed reporter might ask why DND had suddenly changed its reporting format. Canada's Deputy Chief of the Defence Staff, Lieutenant General Ray Henault, was designated to conduct the briefing, so the directorate "prepped" him. Henault was to lean over the podium, look directly (and sternly) at the reporter, lower his voice, and say, "I hate to remind you [sir, ma'am] but this is serious business, not a numbers game." As it turned out, nobody even questioned the change.

April 13, 1999 Following a NATO air attack against a train in Grdelica, Yugoslavian media outlets had broadcast reports of ten dead and 16 injured civilian passengers. The attack, they said, had been deliberate. To counter the Serbian claim, Jamie Shea and his colleagues released a short video segment filmed, they said, by the pilot during the attack. The image televised to the western world showed an apparently unavoidable tragedy. Viewers could see a guided missile steadily approaching the centre span of an empty bridge. Suddenly – just before the missile hits – a train leaps across the screen and fills the target area. In defence of the pilot, General Wesley Clark, NATO's overall commander, explained, "You can see, if you were focussing on your job as a pilot, how suddenly that train appeared. It was really unfortunate."

It has since been reported that the NATO video was a fabrication. The footage that Jamie Shea's technicians produced was actually spliced together from two separate attack segments. The train's approach was played at three times its actual speed. It did not "suddenly" appear; it was stopped dead in its tracks, following the pilots' initial pass at the bridge. (When the first missile exploded, it cut electrical power to the train.) The passenger carriages were then sitting ducks for the aircraft's second bomb-run.

The citizens of Yugoslavia had been aware from the outset that NATO's purported objectives were often difficult to reconcile with its actions. One of the first heavily-bombed targets had been the large tobacco factory in the southern Serbian city of Nis. This massive complex, Europe's second largest such facility, had employed more than 2500 workers and produced some 60 tonnes of product per day. A good portion of these cigarettes was allegedly packaged as bootleg American Winstons and Malboros which found their way, via the black market, into other European countries. The annual loss to the U.S. tobacco industry was said to be substantial.

The Nis factory was bombed four times and not even Jamie Shea tried to explain the military significance of that target.

April 23, 1999   At 2:06A.M., the first of three Tomahawk cruise missiles plunged into the Radio-Television Serbia (RTS) offices, obliterating the Yugoslav state news studio. Sixteen people were killed, mostly young technicians and make-up artists. Another 20 were seriously injured. Since April 8, NATO aircraft had been targetting the Serbian television transmitters and remote broadcast centres, but this attack marked the first time in history that journalists had become military targets. NATO spokesman Jamie Shea had warned of a possible strike against the RTS building, "Milosevic's mouthpiece," he called it, but none of the Serbian reporters had taken the threat seriously.

"There is no allowance for such an action under the Geneva convention," said Natasha Tasic, a senior news director at RTS. She had left the building only a few hours earlier and had been home watching the late night live newscast. When the television screen suddenly went black, Tasic had a horrible premonition. By the time she arrived, rescue workers were already pulling her co-workers from the rubble. "Two of the young technicians killed were actually off-duty. They had just come back into the studio to watch a basketball game," she said. In the propaganda war, Jamie Shea had just upped the ante. No longer would truth be the only casualty. NATO had begun shooting the messengers.

May 3, 1999   For the first time since hostilities began, it appeared that a diplomatic breakthrough was in the works. Throughout April, the airstrikes against Serbia had intensified and the deployment of NATO ground forces into Macedonia and Albania was steadily increasing. From Jamie Shea's reports, the world believed Yugoslav air defences had been eliminated, and that the Serbian Army had been effectively downgraded.

According to Shea, the Yugoslav forces in Kosovo were now out of fuel and ammo as a result of NATO's "ring of death" around the embattled province. There had also been a significant increase in the number of tragic incidents in which innocent civilians had been mistakenly targeted by NATO warplanes. Invariably, the grisly evidence of charred remains would be reported by the Yugoslav media, then immediately denounced by Jamie Shea as a Serb hoax. However, a small number of foreign reporters, including a Canadian CTV crew led by Lewis MacKenzie and Tom Clark, had been allowed into Belgrade. Increasingly, these reporters were able to independently confirm incidents of NATO's "collateral damage."

As the campaign dragged on, Jamie Shea's credibility began to wear thin. The resurfacing in Rome of the allegedly murdered Ibrahim Rugova had proven particularly embarrassing. World-wide public support for the bombing was waning with each new NATO mistake. It appeared both sides were looking for a way out of the escalating conflict, and Russian special envoy Viktor Chernomyrdin was desperately trying to find some diplomatic middle ground. On May 2, as a gesture of good faith, the Yugoslav government had released the three captive U.S. soldiers to Reverend Jesse Jackson. They had been welcomed at the Frankfurt, Germany airbase as returning heroes. The next day, Chernomyrdin had flown to Washington to hammer out a peace proposal with U.S. Secretary of State Madeleine Albright.

On May 7, after four days of shuttle diplomacy, Viktor Chernomyrdin was able to obtain an "agreement in principle" from Slobodan Milosevic in Belgrade. (The Group of Eight (G-8) representatives in Bonn had signed the draft proposal the previous day.)

With the long-awaited peace deal finally within grasp, the following night's attack on the Chinese embassy defied logic. Three Chinese diplomats were killed, and dozens more injured, when three Tomahawk cruise missiles slammed into their compound. The world was shocked, the Chinese public was outraged, and the NATO/U.S. spokesmen were unable to provide a rational explanation. "Sorry, we used the wrong maps," simply didn't make sense to anyone who understood how global positioning (GPS) guidance systems work – or to anyone who had been to Belgrade in recent years. The new Chinese embassy is a stand-alone structure, apart from other developments, and built on what was previously an empty field.

Whether by design, or horrendous blunder, the delicately-assembled peace deal was blown apart. The Chinese government stated that, so long as the bombing continued, it would refuse to vote on any peace resolution put before the U.N. Security Council. NATO officials maintained there could be no cessation of attacks until their demands were met.

Following the collapse of the Chernomyrdin peace plan, NATO planners decided that a ground operation would have to be commenced. To rekindle public support, the propaganda machine was shifted into high gear. Fuzzy aerial photographs of alleged mass graves were released to the press. Almost overnight, the number of suspected Albanian genocide victims leaped from 10,000 to 100,000.

NATO members were pressured to increase the size of their military commitments. Despite a crushing manpower shortage, Canada once again answered the call, pledging a second, 500-strong battle group to Kosovo.

May 22, 1999   At a press conference in Macedonia, Lieutenant General Michael Jackson, the NATO force commander, announced that the troop buildup in the region was now sufficient for a ground operation to begin. General Jackson told reporters that his units were ready for action, and he called on political leaders to give him the green light to enter Kosovo *now*.

The war was entering a new phase and the media's military analysts were already shifting their focus. No longer did they trumpet the effectiveness of airstrikes. Instead, they began to speculate about the best invasion routes.

The Serbs were showing no signs of collapsing under the aerial assault and NATO was poised to up the ante. Later that day, the Yugoslavian Embassy in Ottawa called to tell me that my press accreditation had finally been approved by Belgrade. I had *my* green light, and I was off to the war.

ABOVE: *As the NATO build-up towards a possible ground offensive in Kosovo intensified, Canada committed a second, 500-strong, battle group. Although the first of the Canadian contingents were not expected to arrive in the Balkans until early June, Lieutenant General Micheal Jackson pronounced his Macedonia-based NATO forces (KFOR) ready for immediate action on May 22, 1999. The major reason for the lengthy delay in Canadian troops joining their allies was the lack of available commercial shipping to transport their vehicles (such as the Bison Armoured Personnel Carriers shown here).* (PHOTO BY AUTHOR)

ABOVE: *A housing complex in Novi Sad shows the effects of a NATO carpet-bomb attack. Forty civilians were killed and hundreds left homeless by this single "mistake."*

OPPOSITE PAGE: *All of Belgrade is plunged into blackness following a successful strike on the Zemun transformers. (PHOTOS BY AUTHOR)*

4 - INTO THE FRAY

Subotica, May 24, 1999 (Sunday afternoon)   Until my arrival at the Hungary/
Yugoslavia border, the trip had gone without a hitch. As there were no international flights into Belgrade (other than the NATO bombers), I had to fly to Budapest first, then secure passage on a Yugoslavia bound mini-bus.

Apologizing for the rush, an agent at the Budapest airport had explained that
all the drivers had to be en route to Yugoslavia before 3:00P.M. in order to complete
the six-hour trek before dark. (While NATO had begun launching daylight air
strikes, the majority of the attacks still took place at night and main roads were a
favourite target.)

I managed to secure a berth on the last scheduled vehicle. At the border, we
found a considerable amount of traffic already backlogged in the 400 metre neutral zone, which separated Yugoslavia from Hungary. However, the actual queue
through the Yugoslav customs and police checkpoint was moving quickly, as most
travelers seemed intent on patronizing the six, large, duty-free shops that occupied the short stretch of neutral ground.

Knowing I had a valid visa – along with a recommendation from the Yugoslavian Embassy in Ottawa – I felt no trepidation as we approached the Serb border
police. My confidence quickly vanished though, when a thick finger pointed at

me through the driver's window. Although the officer spoke in Serbian, his thumb-jerking motion left no doubt as to his meaning. By the time I got inside the customs building, the bus driver had already unloaded my bags at the curbside and had sped off towards Belgrade.

A Serbian captain explained to me that I did not have a stamp in my passport signifying I had been registered by the police. I asked how I could acquire such a stamp. He replied, "It can be done only in Belgrade, at police headquarters." Naturally, my next question was, How does one get to Belgrade to get a border clearance without first clearing the border? Shrugging his shoulders, he stated, "That's your problem."

For the next six hours, I alternately sat in the police waiting room or strolled about the duty-free area. As dusk approached, the traffic had all but disappeared. At 9:30P.M., the duty-free shops closed up, the sales staff departed and the police changed shifts.

With not much else to occupy them, the new crew of police turned its attention to me. One sergeant decided to search through my luggage – presumably looking for contraband. He discovered a number of letters written in Serbian. These notes of introduction had been prepared for me by Bora Dragasevich, the Toronto-based president of the Serbian National Shield Society of Canada. In these letters, Dragasevich explained, among other things, that I, as a journalist, had helped publicize the Croatian massacre of Serbs in the Krajina.

After reading this correspondence, the police sergeant explained he had been a resident of the Krajina until his expulsion in 1995. From that moment on, he became my personal advocate. Quickly, a few calls were made, my passport was stamped, and my luggage returned. The only thing left to arrange was a means of transport. At 11:45P.M. this was resolved by the unexpected appearance of a mini-bus crossing over from the Hungarian checkpoint.

My new-found protector spoke briefly with the driver, then waved me over to the van. I was on my way.

Novi Sad, May 25, 1999 (Tuesday morning)   As the mini-bus hurtled along the pitch-black highway, I had an eerie feeling. There were no other cars on the road, and we were often required to detour around poorly-marked bomb craters. All too frequently, a filtered red light would wave up ahead, indicating yet another military checkpoint manned by roving patrols of well-armed soldiers. The ranking officer would quickly check the driver's identification papers and ask a few questions. Once satisfied, the patrol would melt back into the darkness and we would proceed towards Belgrade. (Invariably, our driver would be questioned on the sanity of driving after dark – with headlights on high beam – while NATO aircraft roamed the night skies.)

The experience appeared to be equally unnerving for my fellow passengers who soon began to pass around a large jug of duty-free cognac. As the miles and hours rolled by, the cheap alcohol took effect. Two of the six travelers spoke some English and soon everyone wanted their "war story" or political opinion told to the 'Kanadski novinar' (Canadian journalist).

The icebreaker was the revelation that my first name is 'Skot' which, in Serbian, translates to 'jerk' or 'lowlife.' "You cannot be a NATO spy," said Beba Ugarkovic. "No one in Intelligence would be so stupid as to pick a codename such as 'Skot.'" The bus erupted in drunken laughter.

As we approached the city of Novi Sad, we could hear the distant thumps of anti-aircraft fire. Flashes on the horizon indicated bomb explosions. At the next checkpoint, a young lieutenant informed us there had just been at least three heavy attacks. About five kilometres away, we could see a large building burning brightly.

For the next few minutes, except for the drone of jets overhead, we rode in silence, our nerves beginning to get the better of us. Then, softly, Beba began to sing a Serbian folk song. The others soon joined in, their collective voices steadily rising in strength. Throughout the remaining two hours of the trip our little bus resonated with a seemingly endless stream of spirit-lifting ballads. All fears were lost in the cognac and song.

Belgrade, May 25, 1999 (Tuesday afternoon) As I had no way of contacting anyone, my delay at the Yugoslavian border had caused a fair measure of concern in Belgrade. Before leaving Canada, I had arranged through Bora Dragasevich – a mutual friend – for the Kopric family to provide me with assistance upon arrival. Vlada, a 22-year-old university student, spoke fluent English and had access to a wealth of computer equipment. His father, Zlatan, had spent his youth in the Yugoslav Marines and, in the late 60s, had served as one of Marshal Tito's personal bodyguards. He, too, spoke excellent English, and had turned his innovative computer skills into a successful business. In addition, Vlada's mother, Radmila, worked as a reporter for *Vesti*, the Yugoslavian international news agency.

Such a collection of talents and contacts made the Kopric family a powerful asset. They agreed to provide me with translation services, transportation (they owned a Ford Escort and had a good source of black market fuel), and computer resources (including my own e-mail address).

The rate that we settled on was less than half what a foreign journalist could expect to pay simply to charter a driver and car. Further proof that this new partnership was more of a 'personal' nature was found in the Koprics' insistence on bringing me home and feeding me lunch. I was anxious to get officially registered with the Yugoslav Army Press centre, but their hospitality was not to be denied.

The mounds of sausages and fried potatoes they served up belied reports of chronic food shortages. As we ate, the air raid sirens suddenly sounded – the first that I'd heard – and Belgrade came under a daylight air attack.

Nobody at the table paid any heed and, despite my growing unease, I too, remained seated. Several minutes later, there was a loud explosion followed by a concussing shock wave. Without even going to their window, Vlada and Zlatan nonchalantly debated which district the bomb had hit.

Andjelka, Zlatan's 81-year-old mother, lives in the small apartment with them. Since the war began, she had been intently following the Yugoslav state news broadcasts. As the "all clear" sounded, she burst into the kitchen and excitedly proclaimed that the Serbian air defence had just shot down two more NATO planes. She then caught herself and (through Vlada) added apologetically, "I hope they weren't Canadians."

Belgrade, May 25, 1999 (Tuesday evening) On my first full night in the Yugoslav capital, I received a phone call in my hotel room from *Ottawa Citizen* reporter Derek McNaughton. He informed me that his editor, Bruce Garvey, was interested in receiving regular reports from me while I was in Belgrade. An air raid was in progress and, as we chatted, sirens sounded. McNaughton asked me what was going on. Unbeknownst to me he was recording our conversation, and my rambling answer (once edited) would constitute my first report from Yugoslavia:

"I've got a candle here beside my bed. All the power is down. The city got whacked pretty good in New Belgrade, just across the river here. We had a couple of big raids on the outskirts, and one explosion downtown here.

"The Serbian anti-aircraft defenders are putting missiles up at the attacking planes, but it's mostly just a fireworks display. It's obvious that they're not using radar. They just launch these SA-6s (Russian surface-to-air-missiles) blindly. Normally the SA-6s are radar guided onto the plane and then, once the missile acquires the target itself, it switches to a heat-seeking guidance system.

"But, if the Serbs turn on their radar, they are immediately engaged by the NATO aircraft's sophisticated anti-radar tracking devices which fire defensive rockets automatically. Early in the war, the Serb gunners learned of this tactic the hard way.

"Now, to avoid massive casualties, they seem to just 'guesstimate' and fire the SA-6s into the air.

"Admittedly, it's more for morale-boosting than for effect. In Belgrade, the citizens call it the Chinese New Years. Vendors sell T-shirts with the Serbian Air Defence Force logo on it so everybody feels that they're a member of it.

"Belgrade is still a beautiful city. The bombing has been pretty pinpoint. There are a few major exceptions to that which stand out, such as the television building and the Chinese Embassy. These landmarks have been devastated.

"The people are pretty well informed. Of course, it's a reversal of the perspective available at home. Robin Cook and Jamie Shea are the war criminals to the Serbs.

"As the city is being pounded regularly, I thought I was going to come here after 65 days (of bombing) and find a smoking hole. That's not the case – I'm not climbing over rubble. But of the targets NATO has hit, they've really done a number on them.

"Throughout Yugoslavia, the black market is alive and well, and proof the international trade sanctions aren't working. The sanctions have been in place for seven years, since the breakup of Yugoslavia in 1991. The black market is now an industry and everybody is involved in it. There's no acute shortage of gas or diesel – people openly talk about the fact there's literally private pipelines across the Danube pumping black market fuel in from Romania. Everyone has got his or her source of gasoline, evidenced by the fact that traffic congestion is still a major problem. At the border, the black marketeers made little attempt to disguise their activity. A dumpster has been set up between the Hungarian and Yugoslav border to assist in the process. There are six duty-free shops in a 400-metre stretch, and a huge dumpster where people can heave all the packaging before they try to smuggle it back into Yugoslavia.

"Everyone's right out there in the open stripping down the side panels (of car doors) to hide their contraband and even taping cigarettes to their children's legs.

"Then, when they come across the border, the cops dutifully find a couple of cartons (which they set aside), and people move on through.

"Of course those duty-free smokes that are confiscated go into a box and end up right back in the duty-free shop. When the shift ends, the shop girls line up with the border guards and head off into their hometown of Subotica. It's a very inventive process.

"Even McDonald's restaurant, which is right across from my hotel and one of the most recognized symbols of America, has got a Serbian target sign in front of it. People are still eating at this particular McDonald's, but I've seen some of the other outlets that have been ravaged by vandals during the protests in the early days of the bombing.

"The Canadian Embassy was also terribly vandalized. When the war started, vandals smashed all the windows and concrete plates along the side of it. The protestors spray painted: "Republik of Quebec" in Serbian on the front wall, along with a swastika. The standard "F--- off, NATO" slogan also adorned the walls."

Belgrade, May 26, 1999 (Wednesday)   Beyond obtaining authorization to enter Yugoslavia, one of the biggest administrative obstacles to reporting on the war from inside Serbia was the NATO-imposed economic sanctions. During the previous five years, all international financial institutions had cut off transactions with Yugoslavia. This put an end to foreign credit card purchases and, with no currency exchange at the banks, not even traveler's cheques could be cashed. The Yugoslav Dinar was still the official currency, but virtually everyone preferred to deal in German Deutschmarks. The problem for a foreigner on an extended (open-ended) stay, was that all transactions (whether Deutschmark or Dinar) were cash only.

Apart from bringing in thousands of German banknotes in a suitcase, another

TOP: *The Canadian Embassy in Belgrade was badly vandalized during violent protests which erupted following the first bombings. Among graffiti scrawled on the outer wall was "Republik of Quebec."*

ABOVE: *With the three main bridges in Novi Sad destroyed, residents had to use a crude ferry system to commute across the Danube.* (PHOTOS BY AUTHOR)

solution was to obtain a black market contact who would replenish your finances for a six per cent fee.

Most of the foreign media in Belgrade had not established an underground arrangement and, consequently, they were limited in their choice of accommodation. Only the somewhat isolated U.S. standard Hyatt Hotel would accept payments made directly to their international hotel chain partners – thus providing their own black market financing at a considerably higher rate of commission than their private counterparts.

My contact for cash was a pair of elderly sisters living in an unassuming apartment complex in lower Belgrade. Their niece ran an agency in Toronto where initial payments were made. Twice a month the two aunts ventured out to banks in neighbouring Hungary and Austria. From there, they collected the cash, which had been wired in their name from Canada (and other international ports of call).

On an average run, these two private bankers each brought more than 100,000 Deutschmarks back across the border. They said they ran no risk at customs as everyone (including the police) realized the necessity of keeping the underground (which is the only) economy afloat. For security, their two-bedroom Belgrade apartment had been modified by the addition of a solid steel front door, surveillance cameras and a massive safe.

Once the cash was in place, customers were notified by phone and a steady stream of patrons appeared, at regular intervals, to collect their Deutschmarks.

There is no question that the six per cent commission allowed these two ladies to live in relative luxury. Their exotic parlour boasted a fully stocked bar and a large screen television – presumably for the amusement of larger corporate accounts.

For me, black market money meant a whole range of additional freedoms, not the least of which was staying at the Moskva Hotel. From there, right in the downtown core, I could walk into crowds of shoppers and meet with average citizens without fear of being monitored by the Yugoslav authorities.

From patrons in cafés to passengers on buses, people have been more than willing to express their views on the war – and on President Slobodan Milosevic. Despite their candour, only a few of the braver souls would consent to being named. (Almost all Serbs are somewhat paranoid given the reputation of the state secret service.)

Novi Sad, May 26, 1999 (Wednesday morning)   In the backseat of the car, the young Yugoslav interpreter closed her eyes briefly and made the sign of the cross. We were entering the bridge to Pancevo, the last standing link across the Danube. Since the three other bridges have been knocked out, citizens felt it was only a matter of time before NATO hit the Pancevo-Belgrade span. Naturally, no one wanted to be there when it happened, so it became customary to say a quick prayer before driving hell-bent-for-leather across the 400-metre gap.

Since arriving in Belgrade, I had been impressed by the stoic resilience of the citizens. Cafés were full of fashionably clad patrons enjoying daylong outdoor rock concerts, and all of Belgrade was engulfed in a festive spring mood.

The frequent air raid sirens, mounting destruction and occasional bursts of anti-aircraft fire, provided startling reminders that this was an embattled city.

These vastly divergent images made for a surreal experience. Along with the black humour that buoyed the spirits, everyone took a keen interest in the fate of their fellow citizenry.

The plight of the northern industrial town of Novi Sad was often in the news. It had been pounded heavily since the beginning of the war. One popular joke had it that, upon hearing how many billions of dollars the U.S. had spent bombing his city, the mayor of Novi Sad replied, "Then they are wasting their money. If they'd paid us even a fraction of that, we'd have gladly killed each other."

In addition to the industrial complexes and oil refineries in Novi Sad, its central position (spanning the Danube) also made it a major transportation hub for all of Yugoslavia. The impact of this became apparent on our drive north to view firsthand the damage in Novi Sad.

Once across the Pancevo Bridge, there were only two secondary roads. The heavy flow of traffic, which previously had the use of a four-lane highway, was now jockeying for position along narrow, congested back roads.

Following a two-hour ordeal to travel the 75-kilometre stretch, we were ushered into the Novi Sad media centre to listen to a damage assessment briefing by town officials. They painted a bleak picture.

Having been hit more than 130 times in the previous 65 days, the industry and infrastructure of the city were in shambles. With factories destroyed, more than 23,000 people were left unemployed; a further 100,000 in related industries have also been left without work. (This, in a city with a population of 500,000.)

The oil refinery was hit 12 times, including several carpet-bombings. According to Yugoslav officials, the first attacks had disabled the plant and subsequent strikes created a massive environmental disaster. Crude oil from the shattered holding tanks has seeped into the soil and waterways. Toxic black clouds generated by the continuous fires filled the air. (As proof, we were allowed to photograph the refinery and the still-smoldering ruins.)

There was a tense moment following our arrival at the refinery, when the Yugoslav guard detachment got word that NATO planes were reportedly airborne and en route to the plant. By the time we were informed, the flight time had already elapsed. Lucky for us, the refinery was obviously not the intended target.

With three of the bridges across the Danube knocked out, Novi Sad authorities were now operating a rudimentary ferry service. For thousands of citizens who lived and worked on the city's far bank, the daily commute was a taxing ordeal. Only pedestrians and bicycles were allowed on board, and each trip was filled to capacity. Given the delays, there was a fair amount of pushing and shoving to secure a place. However, it was moving to see that a sense of chivalry still existed, as women with children were allowed to the front of each queue without protest.

As the crush of passengers departed the ferry, a television journalist asked people how they felt about NATO. The mood of the waiting crowd quickly turned ugly. People asked why the crew was filming their misery and several derogatory slurs were hurled at the assembled journalists.

The last stop on our tour of Novi Sad was a suburban housing development that had been bombed in the middle of the day, several weeks earlier. According to survivors still residing in the remnants of the apartment block, more than 40 people had been killed in the attack.

I knew the war had taken an incredible physical toll on the inhabitants of Novi Sad. I was soon to learn of its effect on the spirit of the citizenry.

While returning to the media centre, I stumbled upon an almost unbelievable sight. At 2P.M., on a hot, sunny, May afternoon, in a bombed-out city with no power or water, some 200 young adults were crammed into a booming disco. Watching the mass gyrating to the Village People's *Macho Man* under flashing strobe lights, I was amazed. One of the patrons asked me, "What do you expect us to do? It's not safe to go out at night."

LEFT: Christ is Risen! As part of the Yugoslav government's propaganda campaign, bilingual billboards such as this were displayed in front of major hotels (such as the Moskva Hotel, **ABOVE**) and the foreign press centre.

Serbs were angered by NATO's refusal to suspend bombing on Easter, the holiest day in the Orthodox calendar.

(PHOTOS BY AUTHOR)

ABOVE: *The tiny coffin of four-year-old Dijana Pavlovic is lowered into the grave as her grieving relatives mourn the tragic death of an innocent child. Dijana and her brother, Stefan, were killed by a NATO bomb three days earlier.*

OPPOSITE PAGE: *A Serbian soldier home on leave in Belgrade shows his appreciation for former Miss Canada, Playboy Playmate Danielle House.* (PHOTOS BY AUTHOR)

5 - SURREALISM & SUFFERING

Belgrade, May 27, 1999 (Thursday morning) It was barely dusk when the bombers struck and a massive explosion rocked the downtown core. Less than a minute later, a second blast in New Belgrade knocked out the city's power grid. Following the attack, several Hotel Moskva employees rushed into the lobby bar to announce that the Hyatt Hotel had been hit. Everyone ran out into the street to watch a giant column of black smoke spiral skywards from the far bank of the Sava River. In the dim light, it was impossible to determine whether the burning target was, indeed, the Hyatt – home to the majority of foreign reporters in Belgrade. The Moskva's bellhops and desk clerks were visibly dismayed when a maid yelled from an upstairs window that the Hyatt was still intact – the billowing smoke was coming from the district of Zemun. Like most Belgraders, the Moskva staff believed the NATO air raids would stop immediately due to a massive, international, public backlash, should "collateral damage" be inflicted upon the foreign press corps.

A more immediate and personal concern was the power outage, which meant that I now had to rely upon my translator's laptop computer to input and file my story. Unfortunately, Vlada's portable computer had only enough battery power to compose the article. I would have to find another method to send it to Ottawa.

After first securing permission from the Hotel Moskva manager to use their generator, Vlada and Zlatan disassembled their computer equipment by candle-light.

Carefully negotiating the pitch-black roads, they transported the necessary gear to the Moskva, only to see the hotel generator sputter and die promptly after their arrival. The night manager was apologetic, saying he just couldn't under-stand the problem.

"In 26 years, that generator has never failed, and it's never needed any main-tenance. Why would it break down now?" he wondered.

As my press deadline loomed nearer, I had no option but to telephone the *Ottawa Citizen* and dictate my story line-by-line, using a candle to read my scrawled notes.

Shortly past midnight, power was briefly restored to the downtown sector. With their computer gear still sitting in my tiny hotel room, Vlada and Zlatan decided to have a go at transmitting photos via e-mail. (Prior to the blackout, we had digitally scanned in three photos, which I had hoped to send to the *Citizen* to illustrate my copy.)

It was stiflingly hot, and our work was hampered by the continuing air raids which constantly threatened to (and twice did) cut the power again. Due to exces-sive bomb damage, the telephone exchanges were unreliable. Several times, in the middle of sending files, we were knocked "off-line." At 2:45 A.M. our persistence finally paid off. When the report came back that the photos had been successfully received by the *Citizen*, we cracked open a bottle of wine. For the next hour, we drank lukewarm Chardonnay and quietly watched the fireworks as wave after wave of jets pounded the Obrenavac district.

Belgrade, May 27, 1999 (Thursday)   News agencies covering NATO seemed to have no such difficulty in getting their message into Yugoslavia. With BBC World Report and CNN News being broadcast via satellite using powerful transmitters based in Bosnia, new developments were known almost immediately inside Bel-grade. This morning, the major story on all the networks had been the announce-ment by The Hague War Crimes Tribunal that indictments had been issued against Yugoslav President Slobodan Milosevic and four of his top officials.

At a hastily convened press conference, Yugoslav officials formally rejected the indictments, claiming they were a "U.S. propaganda ploy, aimed at sabotaging the latest peace initiatives." Goran Matic, the Yugoslavian Minister of Information, stated that the entire U.N. judicial process was tainted. "The Hague Tribunal is, in reality, an inquisition which the U.S. is using to deny sovereign rights to any government which does not comply to their wishes," he added.

When asked whether Slobodan Milosevic and the four other Serbian officials would submit to the tribunal voluntarily, Matic replied, "Yes, but only after President Clinton, General Clark, Tony Blair, Robin Cook and other top NATO officials are similarly indicted."

Justice Louise Arbour, the International Criminal Tribunal's chief prosecutor, came under personal attack following her announcement of the five war crime indictments. The Yugoslavian government claimed that the U.S. State Department had had direct input in the decision to indict Milosevic. According to Matic, Madeleine Albright, the U.S. Secretary of State, had met with Arbour just prior to the announcement. He firmly believed that Albright was instrumental in influencing Madame Arbour's decision. "Louise Arbour is just the dangling puppet and Madeleine Albright is the one pulling her strings," he said.

To support his thesis, Matic explained that the indictment of Serbian leaders stood in stark contrast to Arbour's May 23 decision to probe top NATO officials for alleged war crimes.

"Now it would appear that such a course is no longer in The Hague Tribunal's jurisdiction," he stated. Throughout Belgrade, public reaction to the U.N.'s announcement was studied indifference.

For the past several weeks, NATO planes have been dropping propaganda leaflets urging the Serbs to overthrow Milosevic. Many Belgraders feel that the war crime charges are part of the same public relations campaign.

"The U.N. and NATO have no credibility," said Slavica Angarkovic, a 23-year-old university student and ardent anti-Milosevic activist.

"Where was the U.S. support in 1997, when we were protesting in the streets? They were backing Milosevic! Now they are bombing us and asking for our help at the same time?" she asked.

Following Matic's press conference, foreign journalists were taken to a bombsite just south of Belgrade. A blast had struck a Serbian family, killing their two children (aged eight and four), and seriously injuring both parents. The bomb had fallen in a rural village, which contained no industrial, let alone military, targets. (Tragically, convinced their children would be safer in the countryside, the family had moved from Belgrade two weeks earlier.)

As the press surveyed the grisly scene, one reporter took the opportunity to ask residents their reaction to the U.N.'s indictment of Milosevic. In an emotional outburst, an elderly Serb made a sweeping gesture towards the blood-spattered rubble, and said, "The people who ordered this, *they* are the real war criminals!"

Belgrade, May 29, 1999 (Saturday)   Just past noon, the drone of air raid sirens announced yet another NATO strike against the Yugoslav capital. The previous night, we had been hit particularly hard. The city's power was knocked out completely and the main pumping station had been destroyed, leaving Belgrade residents without water. With the streets full of Saturday shoppers, warplanes were once again overhead, yet no one in the packed central square bothered to take notice. The rock group playing in the bandshell didn't miss a beat – they merely upped the tempo and raucously continued their lunchtime performance. A jubilant throng of gyrating fans danced and cheered their appreciation.

When the NATO jets created sonic booms directly over the marketplace, very few customers bothered to glance skyward. Even after two bombs exploded just across the river in the district of New Belgrade, there was little discernible reaction from patrons at the outdoor cafés. Instead, most of the males in the crowd kept their stares fixed on a parade of scantily-clad, female passersby.

On this hot, sunny afternoon, a number of extremely attractive female shoppers had pitched in and done their part for the Serbian war effort – by shortening their skirts and tightening their pants. (Sexuality here has been heightened by the dangers and uncertainty of the war.)

Frontline Yugoslav soldiers home on leave find themselves the toast of the town. Embracing couples are everywhere during the day, and the moonlit parks have been full of activity even during the air raids. Young men not yet in the army try desperately to look like soldiers, to inhance their stature with the ladies. At outdoor market stalls, erotic lingerie and fancy stocking vendors are cashing in on this "hormone heaven" and doing a booming business.

The black humour favoured by Serbs has given rise to a thriving enterprise of gimmicky morale-boosters. Toilet paper with Bill Clinton's face printed on each tissue is a best-selling item. So are tight, white, biker shorts imprinted with the now omnipresent target symbol over the crotch. Jokes are invariably raunchy, and tend to focus on the NATO leaders' sexual proclivities. ("Have you heard that

Tony Blair has replaced Monica Lewinsky? Yes, he's now Bill Clinton's unofficial mouthpiece.")

Given this living-life-for-the-moment environment, it is almost possible to forget the very real grief, terrible suffering and mounting casualties caused by the ever-intensifying bombing campaign.

Belgrade, May 30, 1999 (Sunday)   It was a mournful procession that wound its way through the Bezanija cemetery in suburban New Belgrade.

Hundreds of grieving citizens stopped at the fountain to wash their hands before leaving the burial ground. In the Serbian Orthodox religion, this custom is meant to cleanse away the sorrow, so that it may be left behind at the cemetery. However, with air raid sirens wailing once again in the distance, the tear-stained faces of those exiting today's ceremony showed little sign of having put the recent loss to rest.

Two young children, Stefan Pavlovic, age eight, and his four-year-old sister, Dijana, had been killed by a NATO bomb three days earlier. Such a tragic loss of young life is not easily accepted, even in wartime.

The funeral was not a staged media propaganda event; only two foreign reporters were in attendance. Both Yrsa Grune, a Finnish reporter, and I had independently learned of it through the local newspaper obituaries.

Throughout the service the Finnish journalist wept quietly. As the father of a four-year-old myself, I admit I lost it a little when, as they lowered Dijana's tiny coffin, the grandmother screamed out her name with a soulful cry. The parents were not on hand for the funeral; they were in hospital.

The explosion occurred around 11P.M. on Thursday, May 27, while Stefan and Dijana slept. Neighbours say that, although badly injured herself, Branislava, the children's mother, screamed hysterically for rescue crews to dig out her "babies."

Mercifully, they say, Branislava had sunk into unconsciousness before they managed to dig Dijana's mutilated corpse out of the smouldering rubble. It took another three hours to retrieve Stefan's battered body.

The father, Vladimir Pavlovic, received burns to 60 per cent of his body and was placed in intensive care at a Belgrade hospital. His wife was in a coma, on a life-support system.

With emotions running high, I was a little concerned about the mourners' reaction should they discover I was from a NATO country that participated in the airstrikes. When one man did approach me, he politely thanked me for making the effort to attend the funeral. He explained that, "the people of Canada must see this. They must know what the bombing is doing."

Unfortunately for the Yugoslavs, as NATO's air campaign steadily intensified (with a commensurate increase in "mistakes" costing human lives), it was becoming tougher to cover stories of these tragedies.

Over the past couple of days, NATO planes have systematically eliminated the Yugoslav telecommunications network. As of today all links to the rest of Europe have been eliminated. For now, the lines to Canada remain open, but for how long no one can be sure.

Yesterday NATO demanded that Yugoslav television on the European satellite be disconnected, making it impossible for the Serbs to broadcast images of the bomb-inflicted carnage. With no air travel possible, many bridges blown, roads cratered and rail lines targeted, it has become increasingly difficult for journalists and officials to even ascertain the extent of the destruction.

Belgrade, May 30, 1999 (Sunday evening)   Most of Belgrade's downtown restaurants and clubs closed their doors around 7:00P.M. to allow patrons and employees to get home before darkness brings the next round of airstrikes. One notable exception to this practice was the elegant *Writer's Club* which caters to an exclusive late-supper clientele. Equipped with generators, the *Writer's Club* remained unaffected by the power outages, its kitchen still churning out gourmet dishes. On hot summer nights, most of the diners preferred to take their meals on the candlelit patio where they can watch the anti-aircraft display during the raids.

It was nearly 10P.M. by the time I finished filing my story on the Pavlovic funeral. With few other options for a late meal (one can only eat so many roadside cevapcecis!), I had agreed to join some media colleagues at the *Writer's Club*.

Seated at a table nearby was the notorious Serbian gangster-cum-war criminal known to the western world as Arkan. Since the beginning of the NATO bombing campaign, it had been widely reported that Zeljko Raznatovic (aka Arkan) had reconstituted his infamous "Tigers," a nationalist Serb paramilitary unit that had fought in both Croatia and Bosnia. The alleged deployment of Arkan and his ruthless killers into Kosovo was being proclaimed by NATO as proof that Yugoslav President Slobodan Milosevic was engaging in a campaign of genocide.

On this night, we could attest the much-feared Arkan was nowhere near the

TOP LEFT: *Although he was left disabled for life by a NATO bomb, Dragoljub Tesic still displayed a defiant patriotism.*

TOP RIGHT: *Just back from a frontline tour in Kosovo, this Serb infantryman shows the strains of his experience.*

ABOVE: *Belgrade street vendors did a brisk trade in war souvenirs. (PHOTOS BY AUTHOR)*

LEFT: *Children scampering atop their former home. This photo was considered to be pro-NATO propaganda by Serbian press officials when the young boy pointed his toy rifle at journalists.*

MIDDLE: *The Saturday rock concert continues during a NATO airstrike. There were daily morale-boosting performances at the Republike Square throughout the war.*

BOTTOM: *The destruction of the Novi Sad bridges effectively halted commercial shipping on the Danube.* (*PHOTOS BY AUTHOR*)

disputed regions of Kosovo. Sporting a slight paunch, the middle-aged, cherubic-faced Arkan did not appear to be at all martial or menacing. The only visible trapping of his violent legacy were a couple of tough-looking security types lounging by the garden door. They kept a close eye on their boss as he dined in the company of a very young, attractive blonde.

A trio of guitar players – bedecked in sombreros – were serenading the *Writer's Club* patrons with Mexican music when the air raid sirens sounded. Even as air defence cannons lit up the sky, the musicians continued to stroll about the patio, strumming their instruments and singing Spanish love ballads.

By the time I returned to the Moskva, the power was out across the city and the hotel's generator had once again seized up. A pair of candles dimly lit the front desk and the young bellhop greeted me cheerfully. "No bread tomorrow!" he said. (Without electricity, Belgrade's bakeries were unable to operate and, since their mead contained no preservatives, it could not be stockpiled.)

At the foot of the main staircase were two large buckets of water and a six-pack of small candles. Still smiling, the bellhop advised me that, since he could not leave the front desk unattended, it was up to me to haul these vital necessities to my room on the fifth floor. The once-majestic Moskva boasts classic architecture, complete with 18-foot ceilings on every floor. This was not much consolation to me, as I lugged the heavy buckets up the seemingly endless, pitch-black stairwells.

Belgrade, May 31, 1999 (morning) Vlada Kopric had arrived over an hour late at the local café where we met each day before beginning work. He was apologetic, but explained his tardiness was due to the previous night's bombing.

A Tomahawk cruise missile had landed on the *Yugo Import Building* and failed to detonate. This complex was right next to the office tower in which his father, Zlatan, worked. In anticipation of a possible explosion, all the neighbouring workplaces had to be hastily emptied. Since first light, Zlatan and Vlada had been moving computers and filing cabinets into a nearby warehouse. At my urging, Vlada agreed to drive me to the *Yugo Import Building* to inspect the damage.

I had an old excursion pass authorizing me to photograph "bomb damage in Belgrade." These flimsy yellow sheets of paper were issued by the press centre on a daily basis and they usually granted reporters only limited access to specific locations. Rather than seek formal permission and risk refusal we decided it was best to simply misinterpret the expiration date on my pass. (We could always beg forgiveness later.)

When we arrived at the bomb-site, there appeared to have been some mistake. From the outside, the *Yugo Import Building* was completely intact. Only a night watchman could be seen on the front steps of this impressive 12-storey concrete and glass building. He was slowly playing out a yellow plastic roll of police tape across the front doors. If, indeed, an unexploded Tomahawk missile lay somewhere inside that structure, just sealing off the entranceway seemed foolhardly.

When Vlada and I approached the guard, we quickly realized he was still in shock. He explained that he had been alone on duty at 4:00A.M. when the giant cruise missile plunged into the building. Vlada suggested he must have thanked God that it turned out to be a dud. "What dud? That thing exploded!" the watchman cried. To prove his point, he took us inside. It was as if the entire complex had been gutted from the inside. The building had been a hollow square built around a central courtyard. The incredibly accurate global-positioning (GPS) guidance system on the Tomahawk had delivered its payload right into the middle of this open air garden.

As we surveyed the wreckage, it became apparent that there had been literally nothing in the *Yugo Import* offices prior to the attack. The guard explained that, even before the NATO bombing campaign began, all of the building's contents had been removed.

(This was true of most of the major Yugoslav complexes targetted in the airstrikes and explained why there had been so few "secondary fires" created by the bombs.)

The guard's nerves were shot. Since his phone had been destroyed in the blast, he said he had been unable to report the bombing to anyone. And, as long as people believed that there was a dud buried inside, no one would come near the building. When asked why he didn't just walk across the road and tell someone, he explained, "Because I'm still on duty and I can't leave my post. But I will, as soon as I'm off work at 10:00A.M."

Belgrade, May 31, 1999 (Monday evening)   A lanky Serbian teenager proudly proclaimed, "Our generals say that, if a ground war begins, our forces will bleed the NATO armies white in the hills of Kosovo." From the corner of the room, a middle-aged man replied, "Then our generals are full of shit."

Seven years earlier, that man, Branko Opacic, had served with the notorious Serb paramilitary Tiger regiment. During that time, he endured three-and-a-half months of bitter street fighting in the city of Vukovar.

As for the reputation shrouding his former unit, Opacic dismissed all allegations of atrocities. "Then I was a soldier; now I am a real criminal: I'm a lawyer," he joked.

As an experienced soldier, Opacic didn't underestimate the capability, and technological superiority, of the NATO troops.

"But that doesn't mean I wouldn't still go to fight," he hastily clarified.

A self-sacrificing, defiant spirit exists in the entire Serbian people. Even Andjelka, my translator's 81-year-old grandmother, has vowed to kill a NATO soldier herself should the Alliance ever occupy Belgrade by force.

As a nightly show of defiance, the Serbian anti-aircraft gunners put up a brave – albeit fruitless – barrage against the unseen attackers. When the power was still on, most residents stubbornly refused to adhere to any of the blackout regulations. As a result, Belgrade homes remained fairly well-lit, even throughout bomb attacks. "How else could the NATO pilots see us giving them the finger?" the citizens ask.

On city streets, there was a paucity of uniformed soldiers. So as not to overly alarm the citizens, troops returning from the war front were encouraged to wear civilian clothing while on leave. Many of those soldiers I saw were from either the local air defence units, or young recruits who've been recently mobilized. From their appearance, it was apparent that army boots were in short supply; loafers, sneakers, and even sandals, were all worn as a substitute for proper footwear. I saw one trooper sporting a Toronto Maple Leafs jersey along with his combat pants.

On several occasions I observed groups of combat soldiers fresh from the front lines in Kosovo. Obviously the elite of the Yugoslav Army, they appeared to be both fit and well equipped. Beyond their rugged appearance, these soldiers were set apart by the unblinking, thousand-yard stares, common to battle-fatigued troops the world over.

From the sketchy reports available – Serb soldiers were reluctant to discuss their experiences with foreign journalists for security reasons – active service in Kosovo was a nerve-wracking ordeal.

One of the strangest characters I encountered was a self-described, Slovenian mercenary, swaggering about in front of the Hotel Moskva café. His AK-47 assault rifle had an extra clip of ammo taped onto it, a commando knife adorned his webbing and another was tucked into his boot. A holstered, .45-calibre pistol rounded out his gear.

At about 50 years of age (with at least that many extra pounds hanging on his diminutive frame), this chap made quite a sight. He spoke at length, explaining that he was not accepting any official payment for his services; he "just wanted to kill Americans."

Unfortunately, he would not let me photograph him, insisting his presence in Belgrade was a military secret. Judging from the amused response of the elegantly attired passersby, individuals such as he were rare.

It seemed to me that this character had never been near a front line in his lifetime, and likely never would.

Valjevo, June 1, 1999 (Tuesday afternoon)   Slavoljub Simic struggled to sit upright in his hospital bed and painfully told his story to a small group of foreign reporters. He described how he had been loading a truck at the nearby Krusik factory when NATO struck. Over 43 projectiles exploded on the two-acre grounds of the manufacturing plant and Simic described the effect as "horrific." An initial blast threw him from his truck and, throughout the bombardment, he "was flung bodily about amidst the concrete debris so many times [he] lost count."

It was only when he talked of his rescuers being unable to remove a large slab from his arm that I first noticed his right pyjama sleeve was hanging limp. Simic explained that his amputated stump had since become infected with gangrene, but that the doctors were hopeful they had caught it in time.

Lying in the bed next to Simic was Dragoljub Tesic who had been at his home near the Krusik factory on May 2 when the NATO jets pulverized the plant and surrounding area. Tesic's spine was badly damaged by the blasts and his right leg was shattered. Doctors said he will remain partially paralyzed and confined to a wheelchair for life. Nevertheless, Tesic still displayed his defiant patriotism by flashing the Serbian national hand signal.

With no peace deal to end the suffering caused by NATO's two-month bombing campaign, one would think that the Serbs would be resentful. However, that does not appear to be the case. When asked for his opinion on the war, Tesic angrily denounced any peace agreement as "capitulation" and several of his ward mates concurred.

Crammed into the crowded Valjevo hospital were hundreds of local citizens, only 32 of whom had been injured by NATO airstrikes. (To date there have been 15 such attacks against this small central Serbian city.) Nevertheless, all the patients here have been affected by the attacks. After several near-misses, shattered windows, and collapsed ceilings, two of the hospital's six storeys had to be evacuated. Patients are therefore no longer segrated by age or sex. In open wards of eight to ten beds, young teenage girls awaiting surgery lie next to elderly men waiting to die.

Only the maternity unit and the pediatrics department remained segregated. Children resided in the basement of the hospital where they were safest from the bombs.

Sadly, the situation at this Valjevo hospital compared favourably to that of other medical facilities throughout Yugoslavia. With the federal ministry of health reporting more than 6,000 civilians injured thus far (along with approximately 1,500 killed), the existing medical infrastructure had been streched to the breaking point. To make matters worse, 46 hospitals and clinics had reportedly been damaged or destroyed. As for medicines, the Yugoslav government posted an emergency list of vital requirements on the Internet, virtually begging for international assistance. Only the International Red Cross responded to the plea and re-established a mission in Yugoslavia.

With the economy near collapse, the Yugoslavs have been largely dependant on donations from the international Serb community. Belgrade's health officials said that Canadian Serbs, in particular, had been instrumental in providing aid. The Russians have also done their part by shipping in more than eight hundred tons of medicine and setting up a mobile hospital in the town of Prokuplje near the Kosovo border.

It is inside this embattled province that no clear picture exists. Mirjana Dragas, the Yugoslav deputy minister of health, admitted that "statistics out of Kosovo are non-existant and difficult to ascertain due to the war." Dragas went on to explain that the U.N.-imposed economic sanctions, which have been in place since the breakup of Yugoslavia began in 1991, have only added to the strain on her ministry's ability to cope with this growing disaster. "The air attacks against the power grids have been particularly problematic for us," she said. "With both fuel and generators on the list of banned items even for hospitals, our staff are forced to scrounge these essentials on the black market."

As their supplies dwindled, the demand for treatment increased. "It's not just the injuries from the bombs which is adding to our workload," said Dragas. "We've also seen a tremendous increase in related ailments such as heart attacks and strokes among the elderly, premature births, and, of course, stress casualties."

(As an aside, she noted that the night raids had perhaps contributed to a reduction in injuries from car accidents. Everyone here is afraid to drive at night.)

What cannot yet be even guessed at is the longterm potential health risks to Yugoslav citizens which will result from the growing environmental crisis. Bomb-destroyed refineries have spilled thousands of gallons of toxic crude oil into the Danube, creating massive clouds of toxins each time NATO planes set them afire. In addition, the depleted uranium warheads used during the thousands of air attacks have sparked growing concern among the populace about exposure to radioactivity.

However, for now, the Yugoslav health officials were not in a position to even address these issues as their priority remained coping with the mounting crisis. "Everyday we come in to work and we check the latest casualty reports," said Mirjana Dragas. "I look forward to the day that list stops growing."

For the benefit of foreign journalists, Zeljko Matic posed amid the wreckage of his home in the central Serbian town of Valjevo. Having been in the upstairs bathroom at the time that the bomb struck, he quickly became known as the "luckiest man in Serbia." It was just after 10 P.M. on May 2 when NATO planes carpet-bombed a factory near Matic's home. During the raid an errant bomb suddenly crashed through his roof. Matic says that, for a few moments, he "simply froze in panic."

Miraculously, the explosives did not detonate immediately, and Matic was able to scramble to safety. The 50-kilogram bomb went off a short while later, demolishing his entire three-storey residence. Now Matic can joke about his close call. "Given the circumstances, at least I didn't have to worry about soiling my trousers."

Belgrade, June 1, 1999 (Tuesday evening) I was still writing up the Valjevo stories when my translator showed up at the Hotel Moskva in a state of panic. An hour earlier, Vlada Kopric had gone to the Army press centre for an update on new developments.

The senior press relations officer – a burly colonel named Velickovic – had ordered him to surrender his media credentials. The reason given was that he had aided me in producing pro-NATO propaganda. This allegation stemmed from a brief incident earlier in the day. While inspecting a NATO bomb site that had destroyed a residential district, Vlada and I had spotted several children playing among the wreckage.

Being a novice photographer relying heavily on the camera's automatic light sensor, I had Vlada ask the young trio (who were scampering in the shadows), if they could move into the sunlight ten metres to their left. The children eagerly complied and I shot several photos. At this point, other cameramen and photographers decided kids-on-rubble was an interesting shot, and began to crowd around, snapping furiously.

One little boy, about five years of age, was carrying a crudely-made wooden rifle. Finding himself to be the centre of all this attention, he began to ham it up. Just as the female army major who was chaperoning our tour arrived, the little boy aimed his toy gun at the cluster of photographers. Several sharp orders in Serbian were barked at the children and the major quickly herded the media back to their cars. Nothing more had been said.

However, when terminating Vlada's credentials, his accuser (the escorting major), explained her concerns. She claimed that I (with Vlada's help) had staged the shot of a toy-gun-wielding child for the purpose of further diminishing the world's negative opinion of Serbs.

I had learned that questioning the authority of Yugoslav officials generally compounded the difficulties. However, such an unfounded allegation could not go unchallenged.

It took nearly three hours of heated debate to convince the colonel that the accusations against us were without merit. (The clincher was my developed photographs which simply showed the children clambering atop the ruins of their home.)

In the end, Colonel Velickovic barked out an apology of sorts, threw Vlada's press pass onto the table and strode from his office without looking back. We could continue.

ABOVE: *News on June 3 that a peace deal had been signed was a tough sell to war-weary citizens of Belgrade. Despite the agreement, Yugoslavia would endure another week of punishing air raids.*

OPPOSITE PAGE: *Even in the final stages of the conflict, anti-U.S. sentiment was converted into thriving street commerce. Comparing NATO to the Nazis was a favourite theme of these popular trinkets.* (PHOTOS BY AUTHOR)

6 – DISTURBING THE 'PEACE'

Belgrade, June 2, 1999 (Wednesday morning) Throughout the previous night NATO had mounted several strong attacks against the northern suburbs of Belgrade. Anti-aircraft fire had been particularly intense. Bombs blasted the vicinity of the Obrenevac power plant, and the Zemun transformers had briefly been put out of commission.

At 6:00A.M. the air raid sirens had announced yet another daylight attack, and AAA guns in the southwest quadrant opened fire.

By the time the "all clear" sounded at 9:15A.M., the Yugoslav Army press centre was packed with foreign reporters. The BBC World Report announced that the peace process had bogged down. It had been expected that Russia's special envoy, Viktor Chernomyrdin, accompanied by European Union envoy Martti Ahtisaari, would arrive in Belgrade today for a final try at hammering out a diplomatic solution. According to the BBC, Chernomyrdin's proposed statement could not be agreed to by U.S. Deputy Secretary of State Strobe Talbott. The peace delegation remained grounded in Bonn.

About 100 foreign journalists set up camp in the Belgrade press lounge to keep posted on the day's developments – by watching the BBC and CNN. The three "C"s of foreign corresponding (cigarettes, cell phones and coffee) were in abundance; the air was thick with smoke and noisy chatter. With the city under attack, and the latest diplomatic mission grounded in Germany, there was also tremendous nervous apprehension.

Around 11:30A.M. two unexpected and powerful sonic booms from overhead NATO jets startled everyone. One French journalist, who had just arrived in Belgrade the previous evening, believed our building had been hit by a bomb. He threw himself to the floor, knocking over several coffee cups in the process. There was a moment of silence as he lay waiting for his life to end. When he sheepishly lifted his dripping head from the tiles, everyone laughed uproariously, easing the tensions.

Belgrade, June 2, 1999 (Wednesday evening)   For the first time in weeks, there was guarded optimism in the Yugoslav capital that a peaceful resolution to the Kosovo crisis might be close at hand. Late this evening, Russian special envoy Victor Chernomyrdin and Finnish President Martti Ahtisaari decided to remain in Belgrade overnight to continue negotiations with Yugoslav President Slobodan Milosevic.

Just the fact that these talks were ongoing was regarded as a sign that a major diplomatic breakthrough in the two-month conflict was now within reach. Only hours earlier, the peace process appeared to have bogged down but, by midmorning, the European Union/NATO impasse in Bonn, Germany, had been resolved. The diplomatic mission had promptly resumed its visit to Yugoslavia and, once again, hopes were raised.

The two envoys arrived in Belgrade in late afternoon and met with Slobodan Milosevic for nearly three hours.

Martti Ahtisaari was the European Union (EU) envoy and his presence at the talks, backed by the full support of the EU foreign ministers, was regarded as an important new development. According to a spokesman for the Finnish Foreign Ministry, Mssrs. Ahtisaari and Chernomyrdin "simply presented the peace plan and are in Belgrade only to clarify the details of the proposed agreement." It had been, and remained, the position of NATO officials that the Ahtisaari/Chernomyrdin delegation was not authorised to negotiate with Milosevic. Their mandate was limited to delivering the NATO messages.

While details of the new proposal remained sketchy, according to Russian state television, Viktor Chernomyrdin admitted that the plan called for a pause in the

NATO bombing to coincide with a reduction of Serb military forces in Kosovo. The withdrawal would be verified by an independent commission. The composition of the peacekeeping force which, up until now, had been the major stumbling block in the negotiations had also reportedly been modified. The new agreement would include both a Russian and a separate NATO force, each under their own command. Overall control of the Kosovo occupation would now rest with the U.N.

Although the continuation of talks was a positive sign, Finnish President Ahtisaari warned against premature celebrations, maintaining his position that "no documents will be signed during this summit."

Originally, Ahtisaari had been scheduled to travel to Belgrade last Thursday. When The Hague Tribunal announced their war crime indictments against Milosevic on May 27, the meeting was postponed – and the peace process subsequently delayed by six days.

Throughout the NATO bombing campaign, Victor Chernomyrdin had made five trips to the Yugoslav capital to negotiate a resolution. On each of those visits, his arrival and departure have coincided with a marked increase in NATO bomb attacks, particularly around Belgrade. Consequently, the conclusion of each new peace mission is anticipated with some trepidation by the citizens of Yugoslavia, and this was no exception.

"We now have a saying here in Belgrade: 'Watch out, Chernomyrdin is coming'," said Goran Matic, the Yugoslav Minister of Information. The last minute decision for the two envoys to remain overnight in Belgrade had residents hopeful that NATO would continue to suspend its airstrikes, at least until the talks were complete.

Belgrade, June 3, 1999 (Thursday) It was just after 1:00P.M. (local time) that the Yugoslav Parliament adjourned, after voting to accept the NATO proposed peace plan. Foreign journalists raced back to the Army press centre to relay the news that peace had broken out in the Balkans. Less than an hour later, the air raid sirens began to wail and, once again, warplanes pounded Belgrade. Throughout the afternoon a total of six attacks were launched against the Yugoslav capital.

Even as details of the peace agreement spread across the city, the only reaction from the citizenry was abject skepticism.

There were neither spontaneous celebrations nor protests. As they had done throughout the bombing campaign, people continued to ignore the threat of air raids and displayed a business-as-usual attitude.

"We've been so close to a peace resolution so many times before that we're not going to get our hopes up this time. At least not until the bombing stops," explained Zlatan. Like many citizens, Zlatan has been left unemployed as a result of the NATO bombing. His firm, located next to the *Yugo Import Building,* had been shut down for safety reasons following the airstrike on May 31.

Despite the diplomatic breakthrough, restaurants and bars still closed tonight before dark in anticipation of air attacks. People on the street were aware of the peace agreement, but they realized that did not mean an end to the war.

As part of the proposed plan, for the next seven days, NATO will continue to mount air strikes against the Yugoslav forces inside Kosovo, and military targets throughout the entire republic. Not until some time next week are NATO officials expected to meet with Yugoslav Army officials in order to ratify the peace formula.

Once such a timetable is established, the Serb troops are prepared to evacuate Kosovo, beginning with their air defence weapons. Facilitating such a withdrawal in the face of continued air attacks will require precision, top level co-ordination of timings and safe passage routes for the retreating Serbs.

Given the current status of Yugoslavia's shattered communications network and crumbling transportation infrastructure, the seven-day evacuation deadline will likely need to be extended, even if the Serbs are fully co-operative. Another potential snag to a hasty resolution will be the KLA.

During the past several days, the KLA launched a series of ground offensives into Kosovo against the Serbs. Backed by NATO air power, they reportedly made real gains towards establishing a secure foothold. As a wild card in the diplomatic equation, continued military actions by the KLA still provide a major obstacle to this shaky peace initiative.

After 72 days of continuous bombardment, and with so much yet to be settled, it's no wonder peace celebrations had not yet begun in Belgrade. Even if the cease-fire did take hold, there would be little for the Serbs to rejoice about. Under the newly-signed agreement, Kosovo will remain part of Serbia, but at what cost?

The damage from bombs is estimated to be more than $100 billion, while the combined death toll of civilians and soldiers is estimated to be in the tens of thousands, and still climbing.

No one here can even begin to look at the monumental task of rebuilding this country. For now, war remains the reality.

At the time of writing (11P.M. local time), tracer fire was arcing into the sky in the western suburbs and explosions were visible to the north of Belgrade.

Belgrade, June 6, 1999 (Sunday morning)   Around 4:30A.M., a cruise missile landed quite close to the Hotel Moskva. The force of the explosion shook the building and the concussive shock wave had been strong enough to fling open my windows. Startled awake, my heart racing, I awaited the sounds that followed each of these near misses.

The jolt set off every car alarm in the vicinity and, for some reason, every dog in Belgrade went berserk and began howling at an unseen intruder. (Or perhaps they felt compelled to announce to all their mates that they had survived the blast.)

According to the peace deal announced on June 3, this was to be the last day of the NATO bombing campaign. The Kosovo withdrawal/implementation talks had already begun in Macedonia with Yugoslav Army officials meeting their NATO counterparts in an armed camp. Everyone in Belgrade had braced for a final "mad minute" of bombing during the run-up to the midnight cease-fire deadline.

The first of the heavy daylight raids began around 9:30A.M.; the target was the nearby government district. I heard the explosions from the street in front of the Moskva where I was watching the Belgrade fire department fight a raging chimney fire in the bakery next door.

There was no real danger of the fire spreading, but the choking clouds of black smoke made for an impressive display. About thirty minutes after the bombing, Vlada and his father had breathlessly arrived on the scene, relieved to find the hotel unscathed.

Power and telephone lines had been knocked out across the city, and all of Belgrade believed the Moskva had been hit. No doubt the staff and foreign press patrons at the Hyatt Hotel were disappointed when they learned the truth.

Belgrade, June 7, 1999 (Monday)   Around 7A.M., air raid sirens sounded once again across Belgrade. After 75 days of constant attacks, the citizens were not normally upset by the piercing sound, but this time it was different.

"Why?" asked the startled hotel clerk, her eyes wide with disbelief. "The war is over."

Dull thumps from exploding bombs in New Belgrade and the pounding of anti-aircraft cannon indicated otherwise.

Radmila Vukovic, like most Yugoslavs, was unaware that peace talks in Macedonia had broken off the previous evening, and that NATO was threatening to intensify the air campaign.

Vukovic had spent her summer Sunday in the traditional Serbian manner, a family barbecue followed by an outing in the park. That evening's television newscasts gave no indication that the peace talks had stalled, and everyone expected that the proposed cease-fire would come into effect at midnight.

Following the shocking air attack, word of the war's resumption quickly spread across the city. For the first time, I detected a crack in the resilience of the Serbs.

Gathered around their radios and pumping foreign journalists for the latest news, the Moskva staff were visibly rattled by the latest setback.

Their initial reaction was fear. The June 3 diplomatic deal was widely considered to be NATO's last and final offer. Most Yugoslavs felt that, if their government did not accept the proposal, they would face a renewed military campaign aimed at the total obliteration of Serbia.

This sustained pressure by NATO is now seen by many here as further proof of the Alliance's intention to prolong the conflict, regardless of the cost to the Serbian people.

However, within hours, the fear had disappeared and had been replaced by stoic practicality. In anticipation of NATO planes mounting a major effort during the night, fresh candles and matches were distributed throughout the hotel, and buckets of fresh water were hauled to all the rooms. (Bathtubs in the vacant suites were filled to capacity any time the water supply was up and running.)

The crowd at the noon-hour central square concert was larger than usual, and the atmosphere sombre. However, the feature performers were a traditional dance troupe in ceremonial Serbian costume. I was mesmerized as the large crowd linked arms and, step for step, followed the dancers on stage. Hundreds of people aged five to 85 raised their voices and sang out their national folk songs, effectively drowning out the air raid sirens.

By late afternoon, the black humour that has characterized these embattled citizens returned with a vengeance. Lieutenant General Michael Jackson, the unfortunately named British general who announced the suspension of the withdrawal, has become the subject of jokes. He has been linked to his famous rock-star namesake (complete with all the eccentricities), in a scenario entailing "Whacko Jacko" being physically comprised and manipulated by his pet monkey (Tony Blair) and the elephant man (Robin Cook).

By the time the evening air raid warnings sounded, and the anti-aircraft cannon began pounding out their defiance, Belgrade's citizens had recovered from their shock. Physically, and mentally, they were prepared to meet the next round of this war, and, as promised, NATO aircraft were overhead to deliver it.

Pancevo, June 8, 1999 (Tuesday) It was shortly after midnight when the NATO air raid began in earnest. Anti-aircraft fire lit up the sky over the residential district of Zemun and several explosions rocked the downtown core.

Suddenly, an air defence missile launched by the Serbs arced skyward and locked onto a NATO projectile. A spectacular fireworks display followed, as the smaller rocket caught its more cumbersome prey and detonated it in mid-air. The brilliant flash could be seen across the city.

Minutes later, a second missile, following on the same course, was not intercepted, and it plunged into the oil refinery on the outskirts of the Pancevo district. The fireball was enormous, and giant clouds of black smoke were soon billowing across the northeast quadrant of Belgrade.

Over 20 hours later, as Sala Berisja described the attack to foreign reporters, fires were still out of control and the smoke pall stretched across the entire eastern sky. Berisja had watched the Tomahawk pass directly over him before hitting the Pancevo refinery, less than six kilometres from his home.

He said the attack was "more terrifying than any of the bombings I experienced down in Kosovo." Ironically, he had fled north to Yugoslavia to protect his family from airstrikes.

Berisja explained that, just three days after NATO began the air campaign, he had uprooted his family, and headed for the relative safety of the surrounding countryside. From there, they had gone on foot, to Belgrade.

For the past two months, this Kosovo Gypsy family had been bivouacked alongside 500 other refugees in a squalid work camp designed to house just 200 factory employees.

Conditions are cramped, and facilities primitive. The Yugoslav Displaced Persons Commission provides breakfast and lunch, but suppers must be scrounged through odd jobs (squeegee-kids are everywhere), and begging in the streets.

While Serbian officials say they would like to be able to do more, the support system has been strained to the breaking point. The estimated 55,000 Yugoslavs, who fled the fighting in Kosovo to seek refuge in Serbia, were simply the latest human wave to seek humanitarian aid here.

Since the breakup of the Federal Republic in 1991, it has been reported that more than 700,000 displaced persons (Serb authorities don't use the term "refugees") have arrived in Serbia. The largest influx, nearly 250,000 ethnically-cleansed Serbs, arrived from the Croatian republic of Krajina in September 1995.

Many Serbs living in Sala Berisja's small camp have been there since 1992, when they first fled persecution in the West Slavonian region of Croatia. Others fled the war in Bosnia.

With U.N. sanctions still in place and their economy in tatters, the Yugoslavian government is having a tough time paying its workers, let alone trying to care for the hordes of homeless. (For example, it was only last week that the Yugoslav treasury issued January pension cheques and schoolteachers received their March wages.)

In all the top level diplomatic discussions on Kosovo, there is rarely, if ever, any mention of those who sought refuge in Serbia. They have become known as "the forgotten refugees."

With an end to the war seemingly in sight, the future was clear for at least one person. Despite knowing that the brick factory where he worked had been destroyed by the NATO bombardment, Berisja believed that his house was still standing. He planned to gather his kin and head home to Pristina, as soon as the peacekeeping force was in place.

For those Serbs who had left Kosovo, such an option was far less attractive. Many Yugoslav officials fear that the threat of reprisals by Albanians returning to Kosovo will create yet another mass exodus of Serbs.

As many as 200,000 Serbs remain in the disputed province, and it is thought that many of them will head north when the Yugoslav military withdraws. With the KLA stepping up its attacks, few wish to be caught in a security vacuum.

"Who is going to care for them?" asked a spokeswoman for the Yugoslav Displaced Persons Commission. "We're at the end of our rope."

Belgrade, June 8, 1999 (Tuesday afternoon) It wasn't until 3:00P.M. that Vujovic Nebojosa, the Yugoslavian Foreign Ministry spokesman, could convene a press

RIGHT: *For the past five years, Mladen Ilic has been housed in an overcrowded refugee camp on the outskirts of Pancevo. He lost his leg during the fighting in 1992, and was forced to flee his home in Bosnia in 1994. He angrily asked the foreign reporters, "Why has the world forgotten about us, the one million displaced Serbs?"*

BELOW: *With lengthy power outages caused by NATO attacks on transformers, there has been tremendous demand throughout Serbia for such practical items as portable gas stoves.*

(PHOTOS BY AUTHOR)

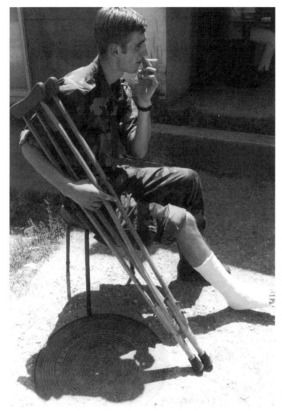

LEFT: A wounded Serbian air defence gunner awaits transfer to the Belgrade military hospital. Casualties from Kosovo were forced to remain in field hospitals during the air campaign.
BELOW: Serbian folk dancers helped restore faltering morale when the peace talks broke down.
BOTTOM: Sala Berisja, a Kosovo Gypsy, sought refuge in Pancevo when the NATO air attacks began.
(PHOTOS BY AUTHOR)

RIGHT: *The Yugoslav Foreign Affairs Ministry was one of the first buildings targeted by NATO airstrikes. Although the structure was completely destroyed, the majority of the contents had already been removed prior to the attacks.*

BELOW: *As civilian casualties mounted, the resultant increase in funerals and hospital visits provided Belgrade flower vendors with a brisk trade.*

(*PHOTOS BY AUTHOR*)

conference to explain the Serbian version of the breakdown in the peace process. He had been forced to drive the 800 kilometres from Macedonia because NATO had denied the Yugoslav delegation access to the international press. The story being broadcast on CNN and the BBC was that the Serbs had made new demands, then walked out of the discussions on the Yugoslavian Army's withdrawal from Kosovo. The Serbs were once again acting in bad faith; NATO had "no choice" but to resume the bombing campaign (which, in fact, had never been interrupted).

What Nebojosa wished to convey to the press was that, contrary to NATO's claim, the Yugoslav negotiators were still locked inside the armed camp that housed the peace talks. He categorically refuted the allegation that new demands had been tabled.

Another oft-reported NATO concern was that the Yugoslavs had insulted the process by sending junior level officials to these negotiations. Military analyst Bob Stewart of the BBC proclaimed Serb delegate Colonel General Sueterav Marijanovic too low-ranking to make any decisions. Nebojosa countered by pointing out that Marijanovic was the senior army commander – a three-star general – the same grade as the NATO representative, Lieutenant General Michael Jackson.

On Sunday evening, when the talks broke down, the official NATO position had been that, after two days of fruitless negotiations, there would be no third day.

It was reassuring to learn that, even as the bombing intensified, the two sides were still actively negotiating. Before climbing into his car for the long drive back to the Macedonian summit, Negojosa said, "It is time for the language of war to be abandoned. It is time for peace and harmony."

Belgrade, June 9, 1999 (Wednesday afternoon)   The farewell scene at the bus station was touching. After the father had briefly shaken his son's hand and said a few words, the youthful soldier was gripped and embraced by his weeping mother. You didn't need to speak Serbian to understand that the teenage infantryman with the weak grin and patronizing gestures was trying to convince his mother that he would be okay.

Glassy-eyed himself, the father gently pried his wife's hands free and took her aside, her shoulders shaking with sobs.

A passionate embrace followed from a girlfriend who appeared to be no more than 17. She tried in vain to hold back her tears and, once again, the Serb soldier did his best to muster a reassuring smile.

When the bus driver honked his horn, the soldier grabbed his kit bag and leapt aboard. He was greeted by good-natured catcalls and shoulder punches from equally young comrades who had already boarded the crammed bus.

Their destination was Prizren, a major staging area for the Yugoslav Army's operation in Kosovo. They had no way of knowing that the heretofore elusive cease-fire was entering the final stages of negotiation in Macedonia.

With her son returning to the front lines, the soldier's mother had good reason to be fearful. Reports out of the embattled region were sketchy, but news agencies were reporting that the fighting had intensified steadily over the past week in an effort to force the pace of peace talks. Television showed carpet-bombs from B-52s pulverizing Serbian positions in support of the KLA.

The guerrillas had stepped up their attacks considerably, and were infiltrating into Serbian rear areas in anticipation of the imminent Yugoslav Army withdrawal. Their intent was to inflict as much damage as possible on the retreating Serbs.

Last Sunday, KLA troops ambushed a civilian bus en route from Belgrade to the Kosovo capital of Pristina killing six, including the driver. Their aim was to show that Serbian forces were losing tactical control of even their major supply routes in Kosovo.

Serb casualty rates were kept secret, but the major military hospital in Belgrade was crammed with empty beds in anticipation of an influx of patients. Many wounded Serbs were being treated in front line field hospitals rather than being transported through NATO airstrikes. Just six weeks ago, metallic dog tags were issued to Yugoslav conscript soldiers.

These army ID tags contained inscripted information such as the individual's blood type, family and religion (so as to facilitate proper medical treatment), burial and next-of-kin notification.

Their distribution caused a chilling effect among soldiers' families (and a thriving street market in phony dog tags for young non-soldiers anxious to impress girls).

Since the peace agreement was first announced last week, the focus of attention has moved away from the NATO bombing campaign and onto events in Kosovo.

As a result, journalists in Belgrade have been pressing for authorization from the Yugoslav Army to cover the withdrawal of Serb forces.

Short of offering cash bribes to Yugoslav officials, every journalist here has been actively lobbying (day and night) to secure a place on the media convoy that is scheduled to depart by the morning of June 11.

Belgrade, June 9, 1999 (Wednesday evening)   Thousands of bomb-weary Yugoslavs poured into the streets tonight in an emotional outpouring of relief. Shortly after 11P.M., word spread that the stroke of a pen in a camouflaged army tent on the Macedonian border had transformed a week of phony peace into reality.

After 77 long nights of NATO bombardment, the residents of this battered capital abandoned their air raid shelters and threw off their inhibitions in a wild party that lasted until the first rays of dawn.

Arm-in-arm, they danced and sang patriotic Serbian songs, flooding Republike Square and the streets of the downtown core.

"Thank God it is over!" shouted 22-year-old Mirjana Jankovic.

It was a scene reminiscent of Britain and the United States in 1945, when Londoners and New Yorkers flocked to Trafalgar and Times Squares to celebrate the defeat of Hitler and the Nazis.

But while Yugoslav TV was proclaiming victory, most Serbs were more pragmatic.

"It is good that my children will no longer spend nights in shelters, but the bad thing is that all this is not for celebration but for weeping," said Srecko Mirceta.

"Victory?" laughed another partygoer. "No, we're just glad that it's over and we survived. That's why we're happy tonight."

Many Belgraders flocked to the city bridge that, in the early days of the bombing, had been a favourite gathering point for thousands of anti-war protestors with the trademark target insignia pinned to their chests. They paraded through the streets waving Serbian flags from their cars as drivers leaned on their horns.

The fusillade of gunfire would have convinced any observer that the war was still raging. Revellers were pumping enough celebratory lead into the air to deter any NATO pilot, firing anything with a trigger, from automatic rifles to handguns and ancient shotguns.

In the euphoria of the cease-fire, a communications overload restricted the city's contact with the outside world. Phone lines were swamped and even computer e-mail services became overwhelmed.

Clubs and cafés, that normally would have been closed, quickly opened their doors to the overjoyed throng, and a spontaneous rock concert was soon underway.

Who won or lost the war didn't matter anymore. That it was finally over was more than enough.

"Thank God this is over, but whatever happened, we did not deserve this," said Svetlana Djuric, 26. Her brother, Ivica, expressed the relief that many Belgraders felt. "I could not wait for the end," he said. "I was sick of all this."

Belgrade, June 10, 1999 (Thursday) It was not until 6:00A.M. that the final celebratory gunshots were fired and the last of the drunken revelers staggered off home. For the city of Belgrade, it had been a night-long celebration of survival.

By midday, however, a sobering sense of practicality had returned. City workmen hosed away the debris and litter strewn about Republike Square and the mood quickly returned to business as usual. Until midafternoon, NATO jets could still be heard flying over the city.

Throughout the peace talks, it had been NATO's position that they were not negotiating with the Yugoslavs; that their original demands remained unchanged. One of the major stumbling blocks had been the timing of a cessation in the bombing. The Serbs had said, "Stop the air attacks and we'll withdraw." NATO maintained they would halt the strikes only after it had been verified that the Yugoslav Army was withdrawing.

It was a classic catch-22. In the end, it took a nifty bit of bluff by NATO to break the impasse. By flying non-bombing missions after the agreement was signed, they could (somewhat) truthfully claim to be maintaining the air campaign. Only when the first televised images of a withdrawing Serb convoy were broadcast late Thursday afternoon did NATO officially declare the air attacks suspended. By that time, most residents of Belgrade had long since recovered from their hangovers and were guardedly taking stock.

The cost of the war had been enormous in terms of both human and material losses. With a reported 1500 dead and 6000 critically injured civilians, there were very few Serbian households that hadn't been affected.

A large portion of Yugoslavia's essential infrastructure (power, water and transportation) had been either destroyed or badly damaged. With the U.N.-imposed trade and economic sanctions remaining in effect and the government treasury bankrupt, few could imagine how reparations would ever be initiated – let alone completed.

As they did throughout the bombing ordeal, the Serbs maintain their spirits with a unique brand of self-deprecating black humour. Now, in the face of this growing financial catastrophe, those morale-boosting jokes have simply changed their focus.

This morning's popular yarn centered on a conversation between two Serbs. One chap explains to his friend that Serbia is the third country this century to face the might of the U.S. military. He says that both Germany and Japan were totally defeated, but within ten years their economies had rebounded and their people now live a life of affluence. "Damn it!" says the second Serb. "Isn't it typical of our luck that we won this war?"

While few Serbs actually believe in a military victory, many take pride in their tiny country having stood up to the full power of NATO and, in the end, forcing the Alliance to concede on several key demands.

From the outset, President Milosevic had agreed to allow U.N. peacekeepers into Kosovo but had balked at a NATO-only force. Although Brussels had steadfastly maintained "It's NATO or no way," the final plan calls for a combined Russian and NATO force under joint U.N. command.

As for the key issue of future Kosovo independence, the man who brokered this peace deal, Finnish President Martti Ahtisaari, made it very clear that "Kosovo would remain part of Serbia."

"To begin creating new states in the Balkans based on regional ethnic majorities would be to open a Pandora's Box," he said.

Milosevic tried to focus public attention on these two points. However, as the Serbian Army retreated north, it became increasingly difficult for him to retain the façade of an honourable victory.

Radical Party leader Vojisalv Seselj broke ranks with the Serbian parliament, maintaining he would resign his seat "the minute a NATO soldier sets foot on Serbian soil." Should popular support grow for Seselj's ultra-nationalist Radicals, NATO's objective of undermining Milosevic's rule may yet be achieved – with an even more disastrous prospect for future Balkan security.

This evening, tens of thousands of Belgrade's citizens were gathering, for the second night in a row, on the Brankov bridge, waving flags, singing and enjoying a full-blown rock concert. It appears that, for now, people here still want to live their lives for the moment and celebrate their survival. The immediate future is just too bleak to contemplate.

As for NATO's claim of victory, it was best summarized by Masaru Oki, a Japanese pundit who has been based in Eastern Europe for the past 20 years. "It's one thing for NATO to say they have won this war. However, it is a dangerous thing for the future of the world if they actually believe it."

RIGHT: On May 8, 1999, three U.S. Tomahawk cruise missiles plunged into the Chinese Embassy in Belgrade, killing three people. The attack had stunned the world and derailed the diplomatic peace process. Nobody in Belgrade believed NATO's excuse of having accidentally used old maps.

LEFT: From the moment the first bombs fell, Serbs celebrated their defiance of NATO through massive public festivities. Immediately following the cessation of attacks, they once again took to the streets to rejoice. In Belgrade, activities centered around the Brankov Bridge and the bandshell in the Republike Square. As rock bands played, guns of all calibres were fired into the air.
(PHOTOS BY AUTHOR)

ABOVE: *The streets of Pristina were set ablaze as the Yugoslav Army began its withdrawal. This building had served as a Serb Brigade headquarters and was torched by the "Red Patch" KLA guerrillas shortly after NATO forces arrived in the Kosovo capital.*

OPPOSITE PAGE: *Thousands of Serb families, fearing Albanian reprisals, gathered up what they could carry and joined their retreating army. (PHOTOS BY AUTHOR)*

7 – REVENGE AND RETREAT

Nis, June 11, 1999 (Friday morning) As the convoy assembled at the tollgates of the Belgrade-Nis Autoroute, the mood among the growing throng of journalists was almost festive.

For weeks, every foreign reporter in Belgrade had been pressuring the Yugoslav Army officials for permission to get into Kosovo. At first the peace talks, then the implementation plans, had sputtered and stalled, everyone had begun to believe that access into the war-torn province would remain forbidden.

However, just three days earlier, a small, advance pool of media had been granted the impossible. Ten carloads of secretly-chosen reporters had been quietly spirited out of Belgrade before first light. They were escorted by a Serbian Army detachment into Pristina. As word spread among the remaining foreign press in Belgrade, the mood in the media centre had turned ugly. Everyone wanted to be guaranteed a spot on the promised second convoy, and no one dared stray too far from the press building, lest they miss a sudden opportunity. Lobbying was fierce, with the bigger news agencies using their influence and cash to demand preferential treatment.

On Thursday, June 10, I was summoned into the Yugoslav Army officials' office and advised by Colonel Velickovic that, as the sole remaining Canadian journalist, I had been granted a confirmed berth on the next Kosovo road trip. (Up until June 4, the CTV news crew had been the only other Canadians in Belgrade. After the peace deal passed through the Serbian Parliament, reporter Roger Smith – who had replaced Tom Clark in mid-May – and his technicians had been recalled to Canada.) As I exited the room, a desperate producer from an American television crew approached me. Of the Big Three U.S. networks, his was the only one that had not been included in the first secret convoy – and therefore the only one not filing news from Pristina, which was at that moment considered the sexiest dateline in the world.

(After I turned down his offer to purchase my spot on the next tour, the agitated producer stormed into the Yugoslav Army office. Pressure from network officials had undoubtedly caused him to engage in such an ill-considered display of petulant anger towards the burly Serbian colonel. It was a mistake. Unceremoniously, the American was hurled back into the main press lounge.)

As events unfolded, the divisive infighting and professional discourtesy proved unnecessary. Late in the evening of the June 10 there seemed to have been a change of heart in the senior echelons of the Yugoslav administration. Word spread quickly that access would be given to every accredited journalist who could arrange transport.

With very few Serbian translator/drivers willing to risk their lives or vehicles, finding a means into Kosovo – especially on short notice – proved to be another major hurdle. According to sketchy reports, conditions inside the city were untenable. There was a gasoline shortage and food was in short supply. No one knew exactly what to expect, and nobody wanted to get stuck without the basic necessities. The Yugoslav Army was just beginning to pull its troops out of Kosovo, and NATO was threatening to resume airstrikes if the withdrawal stalled. Nothing, not even our exit, could be predicted with any certainty.

Nevertheless, the foreign media scraped together a motley collection of some 86 vehicles. Crammed into the vehicles were approximately 300 people, representing some 60 international news agencies. I had managed to secure a ride in an old BMW that was transporting Irmeli Seipagarvi, a Finnish television reporter. She had hired a Serbian driver and cameraman at an exorbitant fee, but they were among the few brave enough to make the dangerous journey.

From the outset, the media convoy was a free-for-all. Everyone seemed to think that it was a massive race, and drivers pushed their overloaded vehicles to the limit. To the consternation of their occupants – and the merriment of those who streaked past – three little battered Yugo cars failed to even get past the highway tollgate which was our start point.

Twice during the long transit our BMW sputtered and died. Thankfully, it restarted each time – albeit with a violent backfire. The problem was the black market diesel fuel which our driver, Petra Jovic, had obtained for the trip. The diluted diesel left many others stranded en route. Heavily-bombed detour routes also took their toll – an old Yugo snapped its axle in one particularly large crater.

As the temperature edged towards 40°C, the heat became oppressive. The frequent halts would cause cars to overheat and, during the slow, laborious navigation around the numerous destroyed overpasses and bridges, clouds of dust made breathing nearly impossible.

(Throughout the entire trip, Petra Jovic blasted music non-stop over his BMW's enhanced sound system. Regrettably, he possessed only one compact disc – a 60-minute, extended disco mix featuring such tunes as Cher's mega-hit *Believe* and Jennifer Paige's *Crush*. To keep from going mad, I began to calculate the passage of time based on song repetitions.)

Just outside the southern Serbian city of Nis, the convoy (if one could still call it that) reassembled at a highway road stop. It would be only 70 kilometres until we entered Kosovo and, for the first time, everyone began to believe we were actually going to make it.

As we had raced through the various side roads and intersections, the Serbian Army had held back and redirected other traffic. There was no question that our 'column' was being afforded a very high level of importance. Several European news networks were broadcasting images live from the convoy and, at the Nis rest stop, a number of telejournalists raced about doing stand-up routines while camera crews filmed each other. To beat the heat, a pair of female Italian TV technicians poured water over their T-shirts – then doffed their tops altogether. Naturally, several cameramen immediately zoomed in on the topless girls to provide their audiences with a bit of colour.

At this point, the whole event seemed to have become something of a circus. However, as we set out on the final leg, thoughts of our collective responsibility had a sobering effect. As the foreign press, our mission was to independently confirm the withdrawal of the Yugoslavian air defence weapons that would pave the way for NATO to push forward their ground troops. Therefore, our entry into

Kosovo had become a news story in itself. It was an odd sensation.

Pristina, June 11, 1999 (Friday evening)   With an ominous rumble, the convoy of Serbian armoured vehicles raced down the narrow street.

From the sidewalks, small children and elderly couples tossed flowers and cheered as the column of retreating Yugoslav Army troops headed home from Kosovo. From atop their vehicles, the soldiers responded by waving flags, firing their rifles in the air and flashing the Serbian hand signal. One could have mistaken the jubilant procession for a victory parade rather than a defeated army exiting the battlefield.

We were witnessing the vanguard of the Serbian withdrawal, their air defence weapons pulling back into Serbia as per the recently agreed-to peace plan.

It was these gunners who had engaged the NATO attackers nightly, and they, in turn, had borne the brunt of many airstrikes.

For the Serbian citizens, these troops symbolized the Yugoslav defiance of NATO, hence they deserved a hero's welcome.

For the next two hours, as the foreign media convoy crawled its way into Kosovo, we fought against traffic and struggled past numerous road obstacles created by the 78-day bombing campaign.

As for independently confirming the withdrawal of their military forces, the Yugoslav Army officials put on quite a show for us.

In navigating our way from Serbia into the Kosovo capital of Pristina, we passed 82 anti-aircraft artillery (AAA) pieces, and more than 40 surface-to-air (SAM) launchers. In addition, three separate radar command posts were scattered among the dusty columns of armoured AAA vehicles.

Based on both the numbers and composition of these units, I estimated that this represented three, virtually intact air defence regiments. In some cases, where the canvas muzzle covers had not been attached, the baked-on carbon stains – indicating heavy, recent firing – were visible. Many of the SAM rocket launchers still had empty missile racks, further evidence of the fighting that had taken place.

The soldiers themselves seemed in excellent spirits – maybe because their long ordeal was over. They looked neither shell-shocked nor defeated.

The mood was entirely different among the long lines of Serbian refugees who had begun to flee Kosovo in anticipation of Albanian reprisals and attacks by the KLA. Thousands of Serbs packed their belongings and clogged the roads alongside the withdrawing Yugoslav forces.

It was a scene all too reminiscent of the many previous Balkan ethnic cleansings: Forlorn-looking families clinging to overloaded tractors and broken-down Yugos.

The reason for the refugees' fears became apparent shortly after crossing into Kosovo. Fires were burning in most villages, all of which appeared to be deserted. Nearly 50 per cent of the dwellings were destroyed, most by arson, some by NATO bombing.

As the Army pulled out, lawlessness took over and ethnic violence ensued. Serb extremists were said to be taking a last opportunity to send the Albanians a message, while homes recently vacated by the fleeing Serbs were set on fire by ethnic Albanians. Roughly 20 per cent of the latter chose to remain in Kosovo throughout the conflict despite fears of violence. (Ironically, it wasn't the Serb soldiers they feared, but rather the ultra-nationalist extremists who were expected to step up their activity after the withdrawal of the Yugoslav Army.)

The first NATO troops were due to arrive in Pristina on June 11, but at the time of writing, controversy and rumour swirled around the exact timing. The Russians' sudden and unexpected move of sending troops to Kosovo had thrown a wrench into the works. One American television reporter panicked upon hearing of the Russian column's advance and began shouting, "It's going to be World War Three – and we're at ground zero!"

NATO had consistently tried to retain sole control of the operation, only grudgingly accepting a token Russian presence.

Through this rapid deployment, the Russians had one-upped NATO and now threatened to steal their thunder. After word got to the Serbs in Pristina that Russian troops were to arrive at 10P.M. on June 11, more than 7000 people congregated in the plaza across from the Grand Hotel.

There was shouting, flag-waving, fireworks and shots being fired into the air as thousands of people crowded the city's main street to greet the soldiers, who arrived shortly after midnight, aboard trucks and troop transports. The convoy crept through an avenue jammed with people, many waving the Yugoslav flag and shouting "Russia! Russia!"

At this early stage, it is still unclear where the estimated 200 to 300 Russians were headed. Initial indications suggested the airport outside of the city would be their final destination. Strategically, it was the most important objective in all of Kosovo.

Pristina, June 12, 1999 (Saturday)   When the Russian soldiers — cheered as liberators by a large crowd of Serbs — entered Kosovo's capital during this morning's wee hours, it was a huge morale boost for all Yugoslavs. They took a measure of joy in the knowledge that their leader had publicly embarrassed NATO.

By midmorning however, the international gamesmanship and political power-plays meant little to the citizenry of Pristina. Instead, everyone focused on the painfully slow (and, in view of the circumstances, almost laughable) advance of the British Army towards the city. The previous evening 50 carloads of foreign press had raced two abreast down that same highway to Macedonia so as not to miss the historic photo opportunity – NATO's first penetration into Yugoslavia. With the Russian soldiers already drinking coffee at Pristina's airport, it was amazing to watch the drama which the BBC and CNN tried to create around the British troops' overly cautious approach. Some defence analysts spoke gravely of the dangers lurking on the road ahead, and suggested troops might have to fight their way into Pristina airport. One BBC commentator went so far as to suggest this would be a magnificent "Battle Honour" for the British 5th Parachute Brigade.

Sitting at the vortex of all this swirling speculation, I decided to walk around Pristina to get a sense of the city's mood. Through the issuance of specific approval forms, the Yugoslav Army press officials had, up until this point, tried to regulate media access. Having staged their last minute P.R. coup on NATO (in particular Jamie Shea, the unpopular spokesman) by bringing in 200 foreign media to record the Russian arrival, the press controls were now completely lifted. "Go anywhere you want," said Vesna Jukic, formerly the press centre's most strident warden. "KFOR is in control now," she added, in reference to the 200 Russians.

During my tour, I spoke first with an assembly of nearly 200 Serbs who were preparing to leave Kosovo for sanctuary in Serbia. Amid the crowd of crying women and young children, soldiers and police were evident. Vehicles were a mixture of anything with wheels and a motor, all packed to overflowing with clothes and furniture. Some of the women were preparing food for the long trip. (Given the state of the cars and tractors, it appeared that few would successfully complete the grueling trek.)

The leader of this convoy was 44-year-old former tailor Vladimir Djecic. He explained that these people were afraid of Albanian retaliation, and gave little credence to NATO's promises to protect them. "They bomb us for two-and-a-half months, they give arms to the KLA to attack us, and now we are to trust them as protectors?" he asked. As for the road move to Serbia, Djecic noted that the police and soldiers were just saying goodbye to their families. The security escort for his convoy was to be provided by teenage boys and old men – all of whom were armed with AK-47s.

With the KLA stepping up their attacks along the main Pristina-Belgrade auto-route, even the Yugoslav police units feared the prospect of pulling out at night. As per the peace agreement, all Serbian Army and security forces were to be out of Kosovo within 11 days.

"Tequila" was the only name which a 24-year-old Serb policeman would give me, but he became talkative once he learned I was from Canada. (He hoped, eventually, to live in Toronto with his brother). He was guarding a motley collection of 29 ancient armoured personnel carriers which were to be transported back to Belgrade. Over the past 18 months, his police force had lost five such vehicles to mines placed by the KLA, but none had been hit by the NATO airstrikes. "Do you think we'd be crazy enough to drive around in these things during the air campaign?" he asked. Instead, like most of the Yugoslav Army's heavy equipment, these vehicles had remained hidden. Tequila and his colleagues, all from Kosovo, were to be expelled from their homes as per the peace agreement and unemployed as well.

Tequila planned to take off his uniform the next day and attempt to join the refugee column with his wife and six-month-old daughter. Others in his unit apparently had the same idea; all of the armoured vehicles had been packed with bedding and other household items.

As we spoke, other police officials were hastily burning a mountain of files. Across the street at the Army Headquarters, a similar blaze was fed by a constant stream of administrative clerks. These fires, behind the Pristina media centre, continued all day but the entire foreign press corps was too engrossed in the snail-like advance of the NATO column to notice.

Throughout the day, Yugoslav anti-aircraft units had continued to retreat through Pristina. Their irregular, and often bizarre, headgear (*Rambo* headscarves were common, and a sombrero and top hat were spotted) served as evidence that their spirits were still high. Other administrative units had also begun pulling field kitchens and mobile laundry units through town. The Yugoslav Army had apparently suffered fewer losses than NATO claimed.

Another startling example of the discrepancy in NATO's claims was the sudden appearance of six MiG 29 jet fighters over Pristina. The Yugoslav air force pilots flew a low level formation overhead, wagged their wingtips in farewell, then headed north to Serbia. Very early in the bombing campaign, NATO spokesman Jamie Shea had told the world that all such fighter planes had been destroyed. In fact, throughout the war, the MiG's remained hidden in bunkers. They had survived unscathed, while NATO planes were tricked into bombing museum pieces placed around the airfield.

Once again, this gesture of smug defiance raised Serbian morale. The Serbs who chose to remain in their homes and soldiers awaiting repatriation orders appeared to be in denial. They crowded into the few cafes that remained open and filled the outdoor market. In the lobby of the Grand Hotel, Serbian soldiers lounged with their lemonades, watching BBC's coverage of the British advance. Seeing the heavily-laden NATO troops sweltering in the heat, the Serbs laughed and asked what all the fuss was about.

By late afternoon, the Brits had finally arrived at the Pristina airport. As darkness fell around the city, Serb soldiers shot their rifles randomly into the air and a number of fires burned fiercely. As Vladimir Djecic had predicted, fleeing Serb civilians were burning their own homes in order to deprive the Albanians of the satisfaction.

Pristina, June 12, 1999 (Saturday)   Irmeli Seipagarvi, the Finnish television reporter who had accompanied me into Pristina, had spent several weeks in Macedonia covering the refugee crisis prior to her arrival in Belgrade. In the camps, she had met a number of Albanians and developed several close contacts. One had provided the name and address of his brother who had chosen to remain in Pristina.

Through a roundabout phone connection (via Finland), Irmeli had managed to advise the brother in Pristina of our imminent arrival. As our hodge-podge media convoy arrived in front of the Grand Hotel around 3:00P.M. on Friday, June 11, Sylejman Bucaj was waiting with a "Welcome Irmeli" sign.

Bucaj, and the translator who accompanied him, did not attract even the slightest notice from the Yugoslav soldiers or police units. Arrangements were quickly made for Irmeli, the Swedish journalist Nils Horner and me to lodge with the Bucaj family.

Due to pressing deadlines facing my two European colleagues, and thanks to the five-hour time difference between Kosovo and Ottawa, I was the one tasked to accompany Sylejman Bucaj to his home to assess the accommodations.

His apartment block was at least two kilometres – straight uphill – from the Grand Hotel. The translator explained that the reason this sector of Pristina had not been gutted or vacated was because it housed a roughly 50/50 mix of Serbs and Albanians. Unlike the eerily empty, horribly vandalized suburbs we had seen upon entering Pristina, Bucaj's neighbourhood appeared unaffected by the war. However, there were numerous graffiti slogans painted prominently on every suitable wall space. Both Kosovar factions had posted statements of nationalistic fervor and ethnic hatred. Interestingly, all these messages were scrawled in English, presumably for the convenience of the foreign press rather than any domestic audience.

Given the horror stories of conditions in Pristina, the Bucaj household was surprisingly plush and well-stocked. As Mr. Bucaj proudly presented his wife and three children, it became evident that adding three journalists to the two-bedroom apartment might make things a bit crowded. Bucaj explained that his wife and two sons would bunk with a neighbour, while he and his eldest daughter, Arta, would stay to cater to their new guests. It was an extremely hospitable gesture, and, given the danger of last-minute ethnic violence prior to NATO's arrival, a courageous one. Four Serbian tenants lived in the Bucaj's six-unit apartment building, including a soldier and a Yugoslav policeman.

We realised that three foreign journalists being billeted by an Albanian might cause some resentment on the part of the Serbs. Thankfully, our fears proved unfounded.

Over the course of the four days we spent at his home, Sylejman Bucaj was able to tell me of his own family's experience during the air campaign.

A quiet, gentle man, Bucaj had been a high school geography teacher prior to the hostilities. He had been directly involved in the UCK (KLA) political movement, and had helped solicit funds for their cause. The happiest day of Bucaj's life was March 24, the day NATO began the bombing. When the Pristina Yugoslav Army barracks was carpet-bombed, Bucaj and his friends celebrated.

The Serbian reprisals did not begin until six days after the first NATO bombs fell. According to Bucaj, it was on March 30 that Serbian police forces approached the predominantly Albanian Kodra-E-Trimave (Hill of the Brave) suburbs. At approximately 7:00A.M., the Serb police, in armoured personnel carriers, opened fire on the upper floors of the houses with heavy machine guns. After a few bursts, they withdrew.

There were no casualties as all residents were sheltering in their basements. Asked why the Serbs didn't simply enter the Kodra-E-Trimave district to evict people at gunpoint, Bucaj laughed and replied, "Because they were terrified of the KLA!"

Following the machine-gun attack, the Bucaj family piled up their belongings and joined the columns of refugees fleeing Pristina. Their destination was not the camps in Montenegro or Macedonia, but rather the southern Kosovo town of Prellez.

Since the civil war in 1998, this region, as well as 40 per cent of the disputed province, was under the control of the KLA. Bucaj and his family spent just 12 days in Prellez before deciding to take their chances and return to their home in Pristina.

For the Bucaj family, that homecoming proved to be harrowing. Following the mass exodus of Albanians from the Kodra-E-Trimave district, many of the houses had been occupied by Serbian soldiers. The family discovered that an anti-aircraft detachment had dug in a 23-mm cannon on their front lawn.

Unable to live in their house, Sylejman and his family joined about a dozen other Albanians in a basement shelter. For the next two weeks, they alternately hid out from Serbian soldiers or took refuge from the NATO bombings. On April 12, 16-year-old Arta Bucaj was caught in the garden by a trio of Serb paramilitary troops. Hearing his daughter's screams, Sylejman raced to the scene. A young captain in charge of the Serbs arrived at the same moment, and orders were given to release the terrified girl. Bucaj was infuriated at the rough treatment his daughter had received, and he appealed to the officer to discipline his men. "What is this?" screamed Sylejman. "Under normal circumstances I would come to the police looking for help, and now it is you who are attacking my family!" In response, the captain, who gave his name as Paule Bratislava, and who spoke fluent Albanian, retorted, "You are absolutely right, but these are not normal times. I have told my men that they cannot have your daughter, but I'm allowing them to loot your home. Be thankful!"

RIGHT: A young Serb passenger waits to board a Belgrade-bound bus. These overloaded vehicles had to run the Albanian "revenge gauntlet" on their exit from Pristina.

BELOW: Withdrawing Yugoslav air defence gunners.

BOTTOM: The trickle of Serb refugees became a flood out of Kosovo.

(PHOTOS BY AUTHOR)

LEFT: *Albanians celebrate the arrival of NATO soldiers in the streets of Pristina.*

BOTTOM LEFT: *British soldiers watch over the Albanian "revenge gauntlet" on the main road out of Pristina. The only time NATO troops intervened in the stone-throwing attacks was when projectiles appeared too large.*

BOTTOM RIGHT: *One of the Yugoslav Army's antiquated, but still intact, air defence guns.*

(PHOTOS BY AUTHOR)

RIGHT: Busloads of Serbian refugees didn't always make it through the Albanian mobs. This badly-damaged vehicle barely reached the outskirts of Pristina.

BELOW: Serbian tractor convoys were escorted by young boys and old men to protect them from revenge-seeking Albanians. Prior to NATO's deployment into Kosovo, the Yugoslav Army had already lost control of the main Pristina-Belgrade auto-route. Daylight ambushes by KLA forces were increasing and, by night, the guerrillas had tactical supremacy. (PHOTOS BY AUTHOR)

Even as the paramilitary police unit began emptying his house of its contents, Sylejman Bucaj was once again packing up his family and heading to a safer locale, his cousin's home in the southeastern suburbs. His cousin had fled for Macedonia in early April, but had left her apartment well-provisioned. It was here that Sylejman hosted us.

Pristina, June 13, 1999 (Sunday morning)   By mid-morning, the British 5th Airborne Brigade's tanks and armoured vehicles were rolling down the war-ravaged streets of the Kosovo capital. Aiming their gun turrets menacingly, these combat vehicles made an impressive show of force intended to quash any outbreak of ethnic violence. However, as NATO planners soon realized, hatreds in the region ran deep.

With Serb forces continuing their withdrawal and their police units being demobilized, the KLA became bolder. Although small armoured patrols of Yugoslavs still maintained a presence alongside allied KFOR troops, the KLA could see that the Serbs were quickly losing control.

At noon, on June 13, the KLA opened its Pristina headquarters. Thirty minutes later, they shot and killed 25-year-old Slavisa Isteric from an upstairs window of the converted schoolhouse. Although Isteric was in his uniform, he wasn't a soldier; he was just a trombone player in the Pristina militia band.

Rade Hrnic was driving a red Opel Scona when he and Isteric were ambushed. Only slightly injured, 30-year-old Hrnic left his friend for dead, and fled on foot to a nearby Yugoslav Army installation. Here, less than an hour later, I stumbled upon the story along with Nils Horner, the Swedish reporter.

By the time we arrived at the ambush site, armed with a detailed account from Mr. Hrnic and accompanied by a petrified, civilian Serbian guide from the checkpoint, three KFOR armoured vehicles had arrived. A huge crowd of Albanian Kosovars had formed, bedecking the peacekeepers with flowers and chanting "U-C-K! (KLA) – NATO!"

Mistakenly believing that British officers must be inside the schoolhouse investigating the shooting, I strode purposefully into the KLA headquarters. They were surprisingly cordial, given that both Horner and I were wearing Yugoslav Army press passes. Bahri Goshi, the 25-year-old deputy commander of the Pristina district KLA, agreed to grant us an interview.

Goshi commanded the "Red Patch" unit, named for the distinctive arm bands worn by his soldiers. The group was widely feared by the Serbian security forces because of its bold hit-and-run attacks. Asked how he felt about the Russian troop presence in Kosovo, Goshi replied, "They have no place here." However, after some coaxing from the translator, he recanted, saying: "It is up to NATO."

Goshi was indifferent to the plight of fleeing Serb refugees.

"If they committed crimes then they are correct to be afraid. For those who are criminals and remain, they will be punished." The interpreter hastily added, "At The Hague Tribunals."

During the interview, he repeatedly stated that there were no weapons at Red Patch headquarters. However, when we finally got around to the shooting of Slavisa Isteric, his answers became contradictory.

"They were people looking to do harm to innocent Albanian citizens. They got what was coming to them," said Goshi. "Why do you care so much about two Serbs who run away? What about the one and a half million Albanians who were forced to flee?" he asked.

Throughout our entire conversation, the UCK (KLA) entourage filling the small office took turns videotaping Horner and me, which was rather unnerving – especially after they presented us with our own Red Patch arm bands.

After leaving the KLA headquarters, we again sought out the British detachment commander to report on the killing of Slavisa Isteric. After hearing our tale, the young lieutenant dismissed Horner and me with a flippant wave of his hand. "We're not here to go chasing down unsubstantiated rumours – we're here to provide a secure environment," he said.

The platoon sergeant, who had overheard the conversation, piped up with, "The murdering Serb bastard probably had it coming to him." By this time, the cheering crowd of Albanians had completely covered the British vehicles with flowers.

If NATO's stated intentions of providing, through KFOR, a safe environment for all Kosovars were to be believed, the actions and attitudes of the soldiers on the ground would have to change. Virtually sanctioning a guerrilla headquarters on the outskirts of Pristina was not the message KFOR should have been conveying.

The flood of Albanian refugees returning to Kosovo had already begun, the Yugoslav Army was still in the middle of its retreat, and the situation remained a powder keg.

Pristina, June 13, 1999 (Sunday evening)   From the moment they had first arrived in Pristina, the horde of NATO-accredited journalists (roughly 2700 in number) overran the city. With many having spent months in the Macedonian refugee camps reporting on the Albanian allegations of Serb genocide, they now felt pressure to prove their stories true. Everyone, it seemed, was trying to be the first to uncover a mass grave. Bursts of celebratory automatic gunfire from the withdrawing Yugoslav forces were mistakenly, and dramatically, reported as Serb "snipers pouring rounds into the town centre."

Sunday night, in the foyer of the Grand Hotel, I overheard a conversation between a British television reporter and her producer. The woman held several pornographic magazines. Incredibly, she stated that the preponderance of such reading material in the (now-abandoned) Pristina kiosks was further proof of the existence of the Serbian rape camps. She wanted her producer to let her go to air with this discovery. I felt obliged to intercede to remind them that, throughout the 78-day campaign, Pristina had been a virtual ghost town, populated almost exclusively by male soldiers. In my opinion, shopkeepers in Kosovo had simply been catering to their clientele.

Angered by my interruption, the reporter asked, "Do you really think that Serbian soldiers were using these magazines to *masturbate*?" I replied that, as a former soldier, I was convinced of it and, furthermore, such material could be found in the barracks of every army.

"You are so naïve!" she snapped.

Pristina, June 14, 1999 (Monday)   Over the previous month, Vesna Jukic had rarely smiled as she herded foreign journalists at the Yugoslav Army media centre. Admittedly, as an officer in the Serbian military whose job it was to show the international media damage caused by NATO bombing, she had little to smile about. Nevertheless, her sullen demeanour (plus her close-cropped hair and fireplug build) had earned Jukic the nickname 'the warden.'

It was understandable, therefore, when she mustered a smug, self-satisfied grin early on the morning of June 12 as the first Russian KFOR troops unexpectedly arrived in Pristina, hours ahead of NATO soldiers.

Jukic and her colleagues had long been aware that this high-level international chess game was in progress. The Yugoslav press officials had worked hard to ensure that a sizeable media contingent from Belgrade was on hand to capture the historic moment.

What was more difficult to comprehend was Vesna Jukic's uncontainable delight at the sight of thousands of NATO-accredited journalists arriving at the Grand Hotel. They had spent an exhausting 11-hour day in the sun, inching forward with the lead elements of the British 5th Airborne Brigade. When this mob of journalists arrived, they were parched, filthy and cranky.

At this point Jukic's diabolical plot began to unfold, in all its gory splendour. Between the Yugoslav Army residents and the Belgrade-accredited journalists already checked in, the Grand Hotel was full. Almost immediately, newly arrived news agencies began to outbid each other for the few remaining rooms. The Grand's regular prewar rates had already been doubled, to $200 a night, but on June 12 these second-rate lodgings went for over five times that. As journalists tripped over each other in the jam-packed lobby, a huge queue began to form in front of the elevators. Only one of the three tiny lifts was working, and TV crews fought to crowd a massive volume of kit onto it each time it finally appeared. The heat and humidity were taking their toll on tempers. Several exchanges nearly came to blows.

When the NATO press horde set out to satiate their hunger and thirst, they were in for another big shock. The hotel had been out of beer and liquor for months, and the only restaurant in town ran out of food by 8:00P.M., leaving hundreds still unserved.

It was about this time that the final hammer dropped: The water supply was shut down. Even those reporters who had secured lodgings could not shower and, more importantly, no water had been stockpiled for use in the toilets.

With thousands of extra guests using the unflushable facilities, the Grand Hotel soon began to reek like an open sewer.

This was Vesna Jukic's moment of glory. It had been no accident that the hotel was full; she was also aware that the other two elevators were unserviceable. As for the city-wide water shutdown, the official explanation was "to conduct routine repairs," but Jukic's beaming countenance belied the truth.

Within hours, word of the appalling conditions in Pristina had been passed to the Belgrade press centre, and it quickly spread across the capital. The running gag began, "Have you heard that the NATO media centre in Kosovo is full of shit… literally!"

Of course, Yugoslav Army officials were also residing in the hotel and subject to the same offensive odours. However, they were content with the knowledge that they had initiated this discomfort. This was another example of the Serbian "inat" (regardless of the consequences), self-sacrificing psyche. It is this spirit combined with a *very* black sense of humour that buoyed the Yugoslavs' morale throughout their ordeal.

The war story in Kosovo was far from over. Serb civilians had fled by the thousands, KFOR was building up its multi-national force (including Canadians) and the KLA had stepped up their attacks. However, with close to 2700 foreign reporters now working out of the war-ravaged province, events were certain to be well-covered. My objective was to try to get back home – via Yugoslavia.

Krusevac, June 15, 1999 (Tuesday)   Two young girls began pounding on the bus window, yelling and waving to a group of Yugoslav soldiers at a roadside outpost. Recognizing them, one of the Serb militiamen raced to the curbside, shouting their names and running alongside the bus.

Tears were streaming down his face; both girls were weeping. After he had disappeared from sight, the elder of the two sisters, 15-year-old Yvonne Jukic, explained to me that the soldier was their father. She and her sister were heading to the town of Krusevac, inside Serbia, to escape the ethnic violence once again consuming Kosovo.

Their father was a member of the Yugoslav Army reserves and was due to be demobilized as per the peace agreement, signed on June 4, 1999. He would then try to join his family and, they hoped, eventually resettle in Belgrade.

In the meantime, he remained at his post, providing security along the main Belgrade to Pristina route, which was increasingly subject to violent KLA guerrilla attacks. The Yugoslav Army's ongoing withdrawal from Kosovo had sparked a marked increase in military operations by the KLA – despite the arrival of KFOR peacekeeping forces. The situation deteriorated so badly that Serbian military officials had to request an armed convoy escort from KFOR troops in order to provide safe passage for those foreign journalists wishing to return to Belgrade.

For the thousands of Serbian citizens fleeing Kosovo, the Yugoslav Army made no such arrangement. Citizens either took their chances with an escort of young boys and old men, or put their faith in what was left of the Serbian militia. Even with thousands of NATO-accredited journalists running around the streets of

Pristina, the story that remained largely untold was that of the retreating army and the attendant flood of refugees.

I didn't think the best vantage point for covering this would be a KFOR-escorted convoy, so I bought a ticket on the local bus, finally securing a standing-room-only spot among young families, soldiers and a few elderly couples. By the time we departed, 67 people and their worldly possessions were crammed into a 44-passenger bus. The British troops stationed at the bombed-out Pristina terminal came out to gawk and laugh at our vehicle.

Things worsened as we approached the main turnoff towards Belgrade, where approximately 600 Albanian residents had set up a gauntlet to jeer and stone withdrawing Serbs. Thankfully, no windows were broken in the hail of projectiles, but it was an unnerving experience. Once outside the city limits, everyone became visibly apprehensive each time the bus suddenly stopped. With the massive load restricting visibility, people would shout frantic questions to those in the front seats as to what had caused the halt.

The soldiers aboard were particularly tense, as they were unarmed but still in uniform. Between the panic-filled stops, there was silence, except for babies crying. After safely crossing into Serbia, everyone seemed to relax, and we became aware of the scale of the human exodus from Kosovo.

The first large convoy we overtook was a column of Yugoslav T-72 and T-64 main battle tanks, an impressive string of 67 of these armoured behemoths lined the roadside. Most surprised by the large formation of mint-condition tanks were the Serb soldiers. At first, they thought it was a Russian battalion, but when they saw the red, white and blue Yugoslavian flags fluttering from the antennae, they asked, "Where the hell have they been hiding?"

Once again it would appear that, in the final tally, NATO's bombing campaign success had been grossly exaggerated. Just ahead of the tanks, we entered the small village of Kursumlija, the first Serbian settlement outside Kosovo.

Judging from the number of tractor-pulled wagons and the volume of refugees, one widely-circulated rumour appeared confirmed: the Yugoslav government was turning back Serb refugees to keep a visible, post-war Serbian demographic in Albania.

However, as we continued slowly along the hot, dusty side road littered with the debris of a retreating army, it became obvious that Kursumlija was just a staging area for the fleeing Serbs. Roads remained clogged with tractors, trucks and horse-drawn carts.

NATO bombers having destroyed most bridges and overpasses, our trek involved many lengthy detours. It took more than ten hours to cover fewer than 200 kilometres. In the 30°C heat, the bus became almost unbearable, with young children suffering the most. But, as we passed forlorn families standing next to vehicles which had broken down or simply run out of fuel, the passengers considered themselves lucky.

Belgrade, June 16, 1999 (Wednesday)   After returning from Pristina to the Hotel Moskva, I began making hurried plans for my return to Canada. In the few hours before my departure, I had to write and file two stories, obtain an exit visa from police headquarters and make one final trip to replenish my dwindling cash reserves. Squeezed into that schedule were several interviews with Canadian radio and television stations. Naturally, my Kosovo update included my experience on the outward-bound bus. Off air, one producer commented that the Serbs who were fleeing, and being stoned by Albanians, were "probably war criminals anyway." I took the time to explain that the majority of my fellow passengers on the bus had been terrified, elderly couples, and mothers with small children. "Well," replied the radio producer, "you've got to understand the Albanians' position. These Serbs did nothing to prevent the atrocities from taking place."

I answered him by asking, "You mean the same way our NATO soldiers stood at the Albanian gauntlet and did nothing to stop the stoning of the Serbs?"

His response? "Boy, do you ever need to get home and be deprogrammed."

◆ ◆ ◆ ◆ ◆ ◆ ◆ ◆

Rather than putting Kosovo into perspective for me, as my radio colleague had hoped, the persistent, willful blindness of the North American media continued to baffle me upon my return to Canada. As more and more evidence (or lack thereof) began to emerge, no one seemed willing to challenge the glaring discrepancies in NATO's claims.

Atrocities committed by the returning Albanian refugees, or the KLA, on the Serb civilians were always reported as "revenge attacks." By using this term, the press intimated that the killings were, if not just, somehow justifiable. Given that NATO's primary rationale for becoming involved in Kosovo was to prevent such inhumanities, their callous dismissal of Albanian terrorism should have seriously undermined the Alliance's *purported* moral high ground. That it caused barely a ripple can be attributed to NATO's formidable propaganda machine and an increasingly weary public.

When NATO officials first visited the war-ravaged Kosovo capital, the ethnic Albanian residents of Pristina hailed the delegation as "liberators."

Ironically, it wasn't NATO Secretary General Javier Solana or General Wesley Clark upon whom the adulation was bestowed, but rather the on the Alliance's spokesman, Jamie Shea, who was held aloft and cheered as the conquering hero.

The Albanians' heartfelt gratitude for NATO's messenger indicates how perception has overtaken other fundamental values in shaping world opinion. Information has become the most devastating weapon, and the media the most potent delivery system, in modern warfare. As the gleeful Kosovars demonstrated, this latest Balkan crisis was very much Jamie Shea's war.

Having spent three-and-a-half weeks in Belgrade and Kosovo, I was in the unique position of being on the receiving end of both NATO's air campaign and the attendant information blitz. Witnessing, firsthand, the "collateral" human damage caused by errant bombing, I was also confronted with the difficulty of filing news reports, due to the deliberate targeting of telecommunications centres and power plants.

At the height of the allied air campaign, airstrikes against the southern Serbian town of Surdulica mistakenly hit a sanatorium killing 23 patients.

As Shea took to the airwaves to claim the mission a complete success, and to denounce Serbian claims of civilian losses, the Yugoslav press centre scrambled to put together a foreign press convoy to confirm the tragedy.

It took several hours to assemble the vehicles and to scrounge enough black market fuel for the trip. Navigating the 400 kilometres (through secondary routes, due to the bomb craters on Yugoslavia's main highways) required more than seven hours.

Following a 40-minute tour of the destroyed sanatorium, journalists raced back to Belgrade to file their stories.

Unfortunately, by the time they arrived, NATO aircraft had blasted the power plant, plunging Belgrade into a blackout. International phone lines out of Yugoslavia were cut off (except, strangely, to Canada and Turkey), and the Serbian link to the European television satellite had been disconnected, at NATO's insistence.

Consequently, the truth about the Surdulica killings did not get out until long after it had become "old news." It was clear to the foreign press corps in Belgrade that NATO had complete control of the information front.

Prior to this, other "regrettable mistakes" had caused a significant, albeit temporary, downgrading of NATO's credibility. The Alliance's denials were almost always proven to be false and its explanations often lacked logic. (For example, NATO *eventually* admitted hitting a column of refugee tractors, yet maintained that the U.S. pilot had verified his targets as Serbian tanks.)

Once the Yugoslav side had been effectively muzzled, Jamie Shea's ability to overcome public relations setbacks was absolute. Proof of this can be found in the Western media's fawning attitude towards NATO in the occupation phase of the Kosovo conflict. The fact that the Serbian forces pulled out of the bomb-cratered region virtually intact, after enduring 78 days of aerial bombardment, should have undermined NATO's exaggerated claims of success. I watched three complete Serbian air defence regiments withdraw from Pristina, and the *London Times* reported that only 13 tanks – not the 125 claimed by Shea – had been destroyed. Yet, to date, virtually no one has questioned these discrepancies.

Instead, it seems that the NATO spin-machine remains bent on demonizing the Serbs, not just President Slobodan Milosevic, in order to justify its unprecedented entry into a brutal civil war.

This will make things difficult for our Canadian peacekeepers in Kosovo as they have already been involved in protecting Serbs from reprisal.

Ironically, over the past seven years, our troops in the Balkans have witnessed the victimization and ethnic cleansing of Serbs from their former homelands in Croatia and Bosnia. Our soldiers realize that there are no black and white issues in these regional conflicts. But while they patrolled the battlegrounds, Jamie Shea ruled the airwaves.

LEFT: *One of the much-feared Yugoslav police force's vehicles begins the withdrawal to Belgrade. A motley assortment of these old armoured personnel carriers had spent the war hidden under Pristina's stadium.*

BELOW: *Virtually anything that could pull a load was used by the Serb refugees to flee Kosovo.*

(PHOTOS BY AUTHOR)

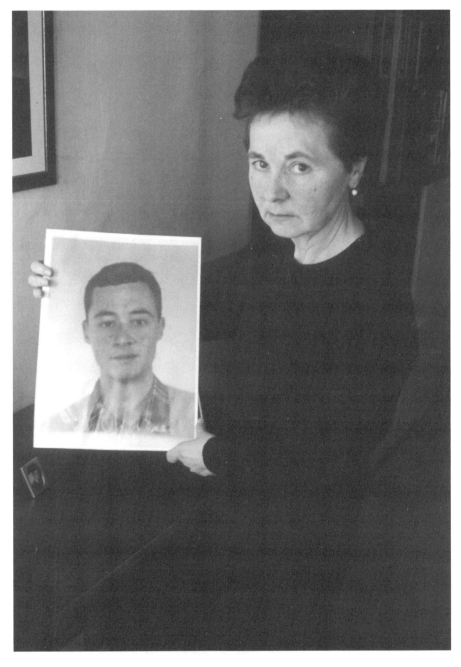

ABOVE: *Ljiljana Popovic mourns the death of her only son, Sasha. An air defence gunner, he was killed during an airstrike against Novi Sad when a rocket hit his vehicle.*

OPPOSITE PAGE: *The war reparations in Yugoslavia are being conducted on a minimal basis due to the collapsed official economy. This temporary pontoon bridge now replaces the three major bridges that were destroyed in Novi Sad. (PHOTOS BY AUTHOR)*

8 - COUNTING THE COST

Vojvodina, November 19, 1999 (Friday morning)   Since leaving Serbia in June, I had contemplated the idea of a follow-up visit to report on how they were coping with the aftermath of the war. News of the early onset of a cold winter sweeping across the Balkans, and the mounting political unrest in Belgrade, had prompted me to return.

Stuck for hours at the border crossing, this trip into Yugoslavia began as a repeat performance of my wartime entry – with the added discomfort of biting cold and blustering snow. Although all of my paperwork was in order – my passport correctly adorned with an official visa, accompanied by a personal recommendation from the Yugoslavian Embassy in Ottawa – the border guards remained unimpressed. None of them wanted to be responsible for allowing a foreign journalist into the country without approval from headquarters in Belgrade.

Several of my fellow mini-bus travellers disembarked to argue my case. (Due to an unforeseen lengthy delay prior to departing the Budapest airport, I had had an opportunity to meet and befriend some of the Belgrade-bound passengers.) It was to no avail.

After a spirited, albeit one-sided, debate, a decision was made at 3:00 A.M. that my luggage could continue on into Serbia – without me. My own passage would not be approved for five hours. Rather than spend the time in an unlit duty-free shop, I trudged five kilometres back into Hungary through a mid-November snowstorm. Unfortunately, the aptly-named Blue Hotel was the only 24-hour venue in the vicinity. A smoke-filled trucker-cum-brothel joint, it attracted an odd clientele – especially at that time of the morning. Nevertheless, it was warm and dry and they served a hearty breakfast.

A new shift of guards at the border checkpoint gave me a cordial reception when I returned. Before I could even produce my passport, the young captain apologized for the previous night's mishap. To make amends, the youthful police officer flagged down a Belgrade-bound bus and instructed the driver to deliver me to the Hotel Moskva – without charge.

As soon as we'd crossed into the Vojvodina (Yugoslavia's northernmost province), a blizzard erupted. With visibility reduced to almost nil, our bus was frequently forced to crawl behind horse-drawn wagons, rather than risk overtaking them on the narrow highway. Huddled on their exposed vehicles, snow-covered Serb farmers were a pitiable sight as they transported their meagre stocks to market.

With NATO-imposed trade sanctions still in place, coupled with the devastation to the Yugoslav fuel depots caused by the bombing campaigns, gasoline had become an almost unaffordable, black market commodity. As a result, beasts of burden had once again become the main mode of transport in rural Yugoslavia.

Since the cessation of hostilities in June, a brief flurry of media coverage of the Albanian return to Kosovo showed the deprivations they could expect. Throughout the hot summer months, lack of proper shelter and a reliable power supply, while hindrances, were not considered critical to the survival of the repatriated refugees. However, as winter had approached, the world had once again turned its attention to the plight of the Kosovars. Hundreds of international aid agencies were co-ordinating a full-scale winterization program in Kosovo, with the full support of the U.N. and NATO.

In contrast, there were almost no reports on the effects of the bombing campaign on the citizens of Yugoslavia, or how they were coping in the war's aftermath.

The first indications that conditions in Serbia were deteriorating came in mid-October 1999, in the form of televised images of massive (and often violent) public protests. Thousands of Serbs were taking to the streets to decry the presidency of Slobodan Milosevic. Fall was rapidly becoming winter, strawberries and sunshine were no longer in season, and the full impact of NATO's actions had yet to be realized.

Belgrade, November 21, 1999 (Sunday)   Throughout 78 days of NATO air raids, residents of the Yugoslav capital had displayed an incredible, spiritual resilience. Few took shelter when the sirens sounded, most choosing to display their defiance of NATO by going about their business as usual. Buoyed by a spirit of patriotic fervor, the Serbs had gamely withstood the aerial bombardment, which was intended to undermine their collective will.

However, in the five months following the signing of the Kosovo peace agreement, much had changed on the streets of Belgrade. The fluttering flags and demonstrations of national pride had disappeared. The challenge of surviving the war's aftermath had replaced sentiments of pride and defiance with a sense of fearful anticipation.

To undermine Yugoslavia's ability to wage war, NATO planners had targeted Serbian transportation networks and power grids. The destruction of these vital resources left Yugoslavia facing a humanitarian crisis which intensified with the onset of winter.

Evidence of Yugoslavia's collapsing economy was everywhere in Belgrade. Squeegee kids were legion, as were street vendors peddling pitiful collections of personal belongings. The flood of refugees from Kosovo had added nearly 220,000 individuals to Yugoslavia's already overloaded social assistance programs. The treasury was bankrupt and could not pay its civil servants. Belgrade's teachers received their June paycheques in October. By late November, they still had not received July's.

Bus drivers and conductors fared a little better, but to keep their vehicles running they had to buy fuel with their own money. The state-run gas pumps had been dry for months, so an entire underground economy was built around the sale of black market fuel. The price for a litre of bootleg diesel was about $1, a 20 per cent increase over the wartime price. A 70 per cent devaluation of the Yugoslav Dinar exacerbated the price hikes, and vital produce could no longer be shipped to market on any sort of cost-recovery basis.

Milk, for instance, was unavailable in Belgrade for long periods of time. The government refused to raise the fixed price of milk because it had been deemed an essential commodity. Yet, without an increase, farmers lost money on each shipment. To circumvent regulations, resourceful dairy operators produced vast quantities of chocolate milk, the price of which had not been set by the government.

In contrast to their handling of the milk crisis, Serbian officials ordered the local distiller to lower its prices to help maintain citizens' spirits during the winter. Despite the promise of an ample supply of inexpensive brandy, many Serbs had grave concerns about their ability to combat the cold.

Over 70 per cent of Yugoslav households rely on electric heat and the bomb-damaged electrical power grid was unable to cope with demand. To alleviate the problem, the power company began rotating two-hour shutdowns of entire city suburbs.

Jovan Mandic, a former section chief of Serbia's electricity system, believed that even these measures would not prevent a collapse of the system.

"It is not a matter of if, but rather, when, it will fail," said Mandic. "For years the government neglected to invest in renewing our electrical infrastructure, which was already crumbling. The NATO campaign just finished it off."

Mandic cited the 40,000 Serbian electrical workers who were able to keep restoring power during the bombardments as "world experts in damage control."

"They had over seven years of troubleshooting experience to draw upon before the bombs fell," Mandic said. "But you can only pull so many rabbits out of the same hat."

Serbs living in older residences, which have fireplaces, have been frantically trying to clean their long-unused chimneys. In addition to many chimney fires evident around town (including one at the French Embassy), there was a growing demand for the age-old trade of chimney sweeps.

One thing not in short supply in Belgrade was policemen. As part of the Kosovo peace agreement, Yugoslavia agreed to withdraw its military and police personnel from the disputed region.

Most of the 17,000 policemen withdrawn were from Kosovo and they, along with their families, were, essentially, refugees. For the sake of appearances, Yugoslav President Slobodan Milosevic said the security officers would soon be redeployed into Kosovo. As a result, the Kosovar officers were absorbed onto the payrolls of station houses throughout Yugoslavia.

Underemployed, police seemed to be guarding every lamp post in Belgrade.

With so many men on the beat, no minor infraction went unchallenged. Since NATO and President Bill Clinton no longer inspired the Serb's black humour, the police quickly became the popular new target.

Question: What do you see when you look into the eyes of a policeman? Answer: The back of his head.

Despite the jokes and public protests, which continued nightly but on an ever-diminishing basis, little real challenge was being mounted against the Belgrade authorities.

"People simply don't have the energy any more," said Pavle Opacic, a former army sergeant who continued to attend demonstrations.

"During the war we lived each day to the fullest because we were unsure of our future. Now, regrettably, that future seems to be a bleak certainty."

Novi Sad, November 23, 1999 (Tuesday)   Winter's first major snowfall hit northern Serbia late yesterday. It had stopped by this morning, but in the city of Novi Sad, rush hour traffic had difficulty negotiating in the slush.

The primary congestion was at the icy approaches to the single pontoon bridge over the Danube River, which connected the southern suburbs with the northern downtown core.

During the early stages of the bombing campaign, NATO had destroyed Novi Sad's three permanent bridges, virtually cutting Yugoslavia's logistical support in two. The Serbians had established an improvised ferry system to replace the lost bridges.

Immediately after the Kosovo peace agreement came into effect, the destroyed bridges of Novi Sad were touted as a symbol of the Yugoslav government's commitment to rebuilding their country's shattered infrastructure. In one of his rare postwar public appearances, President Milosevic announced, from the rubble of the Varadinski Bridge, that a replacement span would be in operation by September.

"Unfortunately for our citizens, the decision to proceed with a temporary pontoon bridge was based purely on political opportunism," explained Aleksander Ivkovac, a spokesman for the city of Novi Sad. "The option we were forced to accept was not suitable for our longterm needs, nor was it the cheapest solution." Novi Sad city officials negotiated a separate deal with the Austrian government, in which the Austrians would provide a gift in the form of a sectional bridge and their engineering expertise.

The plan fell through when the Central Belgrade government of Slobodan Milosevic refused to grant the Austrian engineers entry visas. Instead, the central government's pontoon bridge option was pushed ahead at a projected cost of $2 million.

"This was done out of shortsighted and petty political spite," said Ivkovac, "because Novi Sad is controlled by the opposition party."

To hit the September target date within budget, the requisitioned construction workers had to work for less than minimum wage and put in unpaid overtime.

At the opening ceremony, to compensate these workers for their extra effort, each was awarded a national certificate of merit. Milosevic did not attend the ribbon cutting, but he did send an oversized portrait of himself. Many disgruntled workers screamed obscenities at the photo and offered to trade their certificates of merit for decent wages.

Because it was one of the most heavily bombed cities, Novi Sad now suffers from the highest rate of unemployment. The major refinery and manufacturing plants were all put out of commission, placing more than 60,000 workers (in a city of 300,000) onto what is known as "forced leave."

Under this arrangement, workers are supposed to be paid even though they are unemployed. With the national treasury virtually bankrupt, and so much of the workforce unproductive, there is simply no money to cover paycheques.

"Do you have any money today?" is the most frequent question asked of banks these days, explained Gordana Chomic, a Novi Sad economist. "You have to understand that we no longer have an economy in the traditional sense. With the manufacturing and trade-related jobs eliminated, Novi Sad exists on a service industry that is dependent upon a clientele without money."

Chomic believes it will take massive foreign investment to rebuild the basic infrastructure.

"We all realize that such international assistance will not occur without a change in our current government," said Chomic. "In the meantime, it's tough to put the war behind us so long as it continues to rob us of our future."

For many Serbians, the NATO air campaign has taken away more than just dreams of prosperity.

Shortly after 11 A.M. on June 1, Ljiljana Popovic heard the knock that every soldier's family dreads in wartime. At her door stood four solemn officers of the

Yugoslav Army.

They had come to deliver the news that, at 1 A.M. that morning, her 26-year-old son, Sasha, had been killed by a NATO rocket while on duty. Sasha had been attached to an anti-aircraft missile battery on the outskirts of his hometown, Novi Sad.

An only son, Sasha Popovic had been his mother's pride and joy. He was a gifted student, a member of Mensa and already a leading expert in the field of informatics. His university education and fluency in English exempted Popovic from military mobilization last spring. However, following the bombing of his hometown bridges, he had volunteered to serve as a private soldier.

On the night he was killed, NATO had mounted a 50-plane raid against Novi Sad. Since Sasha's antiquated missile launcher was not radar-equipped, the Yugoslav Army has surmised that the direct hit on his vehicle was facilitated by NATO special forces troops. These soldiers would have been operating behind the Yugoslav lines using sophisticated laser guidance devices.

"With my husband already dead, Sasha was all I had," said Ljiljana Popovic. "I now live only for his memory."

Belgrade, November 25, 1999 (Thursday)   The Yugoslav Foreign Ministry had been one of the first targets pounded by NATO bombers in downtown Belgrade. Tomahawk cruise missiles had virtually destroyed the main building, and the massive detonations had shattered windows and crumbled masonry in surrounding structures. Seven minutes after the attacks, repairs had begun on the secondary buildings, while the headquarters remained a vacant hulk. Inside the remaining facilities, the Foreign Ministry doubled up on occupancy, and attempted to conduct its affairs amid ongoing construction. Under these conditions, I met with Bojan Bugarcic, the Senior Advisor on International Affairs to Yugoslav President Milosevic.

Bugarcic's office was freezing cold – the windows consisting of plastic sheets and tape. His office furniture was an odd, ragged mixture of salvaged chairs and tables, and a thin layer of dust (from the recent renovations) coated everything in the room.

After apologizing for the mess, Bugarcic proceeded to provide me with some rather candid commentary on a number of touchy issues. Having spent several years in Washington, his English was excellent and he did not engage in the mandatory history lesson/propaganda harangue.

Bugarcic had been at the centre of all the diplomatic discussions prior to, and during, the bombing campaign. He dismissed the notion that the Yugoslav government had signed the peace deal to avoid a ground war with NATO. "We would have welcomed the opportunity to at least fire back at them," said Bugarcic.

According to him, the real incentive to sign the agreement was the realization that NATO planners had run out of fixed military targets. They had destroyed most of the Yugoslav Army's permanent facilities, albeit without seriously hampering field forces. "The only option they had was to increase the attacks on civilians and vital infrastructure," Bugarcic said. "We knew that NATO was running out of smart weaponry and that they were increasingly using conventional carpet-bombing. The records show that in the last few days of the war the number of civilian casualties we suffered jumped dramatically."

Bugarcic was surprisingly forthright in admitting the inadequacies of the Yugoslav Air Defences. "Our guns and missiles could only reach up to 10,000 feet and their aircraft never came below 20,000 feet – except for the Stealth bomber, but that's a different story," said Bugarcic.

He said that, throughout the war, a tremendous, and extremely effective, propaganda campaign had been mounted by the Serbian military. The aim was to keep the populace believing their forces were mounting a spirited defence.

Using the state broadcaster, unofficial "Russian intelligence" web pages and Army communiqués, the deception had been so successful that many people were fooled. My 22-year-old translator, Vlada Kopric, was one example. While he vehemently denounced the government-controlled RTS media network as spouting "pure lies," his explorations on the Internet had led him to the bogus Russian intelligence site. As a result, up until my November interview with Bugarcic, Vlada had truly believed that the Serbian military had successfully shot down 78 NATO aircraft.

He was devastated when he learned the truth; that only the F-117 Stealth plane had met such a fate.

Slankamen, Serbia, November 25, 1999 (Thursday)   Situated on a picturesque stretch of the Danube's south bank, Slankamen was once a popular Serbian tourist destination. However, with the strife created by the break-up of the Yugoslav Federation in 1991, and the imposition of international economic sanctions, the holiday makers have disappeared. In their wake, Slankamen's primary function has been to house the broken human beings who provide a living testimony to the horror and tragedy of war.

The town's University Clinic, which specializes in the longterm treatment of paraplegics and the chronically disabled, is both primitive and overcrowded. Nevertheless, it is still functional and there is a long list of severely disabled patients waiting to be admitted.

In one of the congested wards, a mother was spoon-feeding porridge to her 26-year-old son. Micic Zeljko had been a lieutenant in a Serbian air defence regiment serving in Kosovo. He was badly wounded in March, when a NATO rocket destroyed his radar control truck. After months in a coma, Lieutenant Zeljko has now recovered to the point he can ingest food. However, he remains blind, paralysed and unable to speak. His mother, Jovanka, has remained at his bedside throughout his hospitalization.

Through tears, she explained young Zeljko had been married in September 1998, and that his wife had given birth to their baby daughter six weeks ago. "He will probably never know that he is a father," said Dr. Radenko Tadic, the Yugoslav senior military neurosurgeon at the clinic.

In the next room, a tall, lanky man tried to shuffle into the hallway. With his entire right side paralysed, he lurched in a macabre fashion. Lieutenant Milan Mianjovic had been a tank commander whose armoured vehicle struck a landmine in Kosovo. The rest of his crew had been killed in the blast and Mianjovic considered himself lucky to be alive. The doctors explain that, physically, the 26-year-old officer has made remarkable progress, but the trauma of his head wound has left him amnesiac and simple. He now reacts with childlike, emotional responses and has blocked out all memories of his military life.

One of Mianjovic's roommates is Peric Sladjan, a 25-year-old reservist from Obilic, Kosovo. Sitting in his wheelchair, he describes how he had been called up for duty on March 24, 1999, in response to the NATO air raids. His unit's task had been to stand guard at the Red Cross humanitarian aid centre in his village. Two days after his recall, an Albanian gunman opened fire in an ambush and Sladjan was hit three times. Bullets struck him in the left arm, the lungs and one shattered his spinal cord. To his horror, Sladjan recognized his assailant as his next-door neighbour. "We played together as children," he said.

Sladjan's family fled Kosovo when NATO troops arrived in June and they now live as refugees in Slankamen. "Given Sladjan's level of recovery, under normal circumstances we would release him to his home," said Dr. Tadic. "Unfortunately, he must stay here until he has a home to go to."

The Slankamen clinic is not only a treatment centre for military casualties, nor is it only Serbs who are receiving care here. Young Nada Matanovic's family were Albanian immigrants in Kosovo. Her parents had been reluctant to leave Kosovo at the start of the NATO air campaign in March, however, when the bombing intensified to the point they no longer felt safe, they decided to leave. Nada and her mother were aboard an overcrowded bus heading to the relative safety of Montenegro on May 3, when an airstrike occurred. Just outside the town of Pec, cluster bombs fell all around their vehicle. Sitting beside the window, Nada took the full impact of one bomb. Her spine was shattered. As people in the bus screamed and died around them, Nada's mother pulled her to safety.

It took more than an hour for the ambulances to arrive and it took a further two days to transfer Nada to the neurological specialists in Belgrade. Six months later, she still has a bomb splinter lodged in her spinal cord and has no feeling below the waist. At the Slankamen clinic, she is trying to finish her high school diploma, in hopes of one day living a normal life. Like Sladjan, Nada cannot be sent home either, as her parents are currently lodged in a Montenegrin refugee camp. She hasn't seen them since June.

There are currently 380 patients housed at the Slankamen facility. "But this represents just one tip of many icebergs," said Dr. Tadic. "During the eight years of conflict in Yugoslavia, the military hospital in Belgrade has performed over 15,000 operations on wounded soldiers. "There are another 800 physically disabled soldiers housed at the University Clinic and, wherever possible, the injured have been sent to facilities near their home towns."

Tadic would not comment specifically on the number of soldiers killed during the fighting in Kosovo, but he acknowledged there had been a 35 to 50 per cent mortality rate among those wounded. The main reason for this high death rate was that Serbs could not use helicopters to evacuate their casualties. As NATO aircraft had complete dominance of the sky, medevacs had to be conducted over the largely destroyed road system. With an average transit time of 12 to 18 hours, many of the wounded died en route.

The civilian toll from the NATO air campaign has been listed by the Yugoslav authorities at more than 1800 dead, with another 2000 permanently disabled.

Meanwhile, in clinics such as Slankamen's, the number continues to climb. In the past three weeks, Dr. Tadic has had two of his patients die. Their hospital beds were quickly changed, and then filled.

Pristina, November 26, 1999 (Friday morning)   There were 86 passengers crammed aboard the 44-seat bus by the time we reached the administrative boundary that separates Serbia from Kosovo.

Due to the still heavily-cratered roads, it had taken us more than three hours to travel the 80 kilometres from the central Serbian city of Nis. Along the route, Kosovar refugees had continued to hail and board the bus until the driver could no longer close the door. Many of the Serbs were venturing back to their homes for the first time since they had fled in June. Understandably, apprehensions ran high. Rumours were rife about conditions in Kosovo, and many speculated as to whether their homesteads could be rendered habitable in time for winter.

Just outside the village of Merdare we were halted at the NATO Kosovo force (KFOR) checkpoint. Here we were to meet an armoured escort vehicle for the passage into Pristina – dubbed the "Coca-Cola patrol" by local Serbs. By pure coincidence, our assigned escort turned out to be a Canadian detachment from the Edmonton-based Lord Strathcona's Horse. Despite the presence of their armoured personnel carrier, our bus was twice met with a fusillade of stones. On both occasions, the culprits were Albanian schoolboys. Sergeant Colin Dunn, the Canadian escort commander, said such attacks were routine.

"There's not much we can do about it," he explained. "The Albanians know the bus schedules and they recognize the vehicles."

One solution suggested to the Serbs was to paint their buses a different colour and to remove their license plates. That advice came from KFOR commander General Klaus Reinhart, in a memo to the Pristina-based Committee for Cooperation. For safety reasons, this official delegation from the Federal Republic of Yugoslavia is itself hidden in an unmarked office guarded by British soldiers.

The diplomats do not venture onto the streets of Pristina. They take all of their meals at an improvised restaurant built in their offices; many sleep on mats under their desks.

Stanimar Vukicevic, the Yugoslav ambassador who heads the Committee for Cooperation, claims that the Serbian Kosovars have "been ghettoized by NATO's inability to provide a secure environment."

LEFT: There are an estimated 90,000 Serbs still living in Kosovo; this represents less than 40 per cent of the prewar statistics. Scattered around the province in tiny enclaves, these Serbs rely heavily upon the presence of NATO soldiers to protect them from the one million to 1.3 million Albanian Kosovars. Despite the deployment of 50,000 peacekeepers into this war-torn region, the violence continues unabated. Since NATO arrived in June 1999, there have been over 700 murders and twice that number of disappearances.

BELOW: Canada has provided over 2400 military personnel to the Kosovo peacekeeping force since 1999. Their prior experience in the Balkans – and commitment to impartiality – has made them a valuable asset.

(PHOTOS BY AUTHOR)

Housed at a small neurological clinic in Slankamen are the broken remains of a violent air campaign.

RIGHT: *Fifteen-year-old Nada Matanovic's spine was shattered when NATO aircraft targetted her bus in Kosovo. She will remain paralyzed for the rest of her life.*

BELOW: *Newly-married, Micic Zeljko, an air defence officer, was badly wounded by an anti-radar rocket. Blind and paralyzed, he receives daily care from his mother, while his young wife cares for the daughter he has never seen.*

(PHOTOS BY AUTHOR)

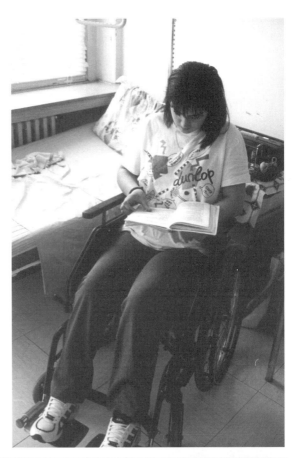

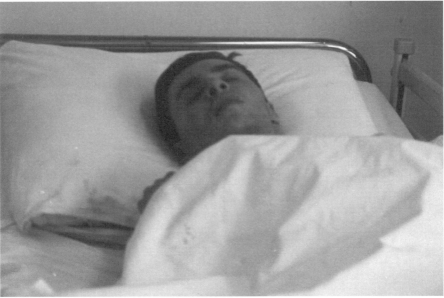

LEFT: *Canadian soldiers of the Princess Patricia's Canadian Light Infantry and the Lord Strathcona's Horse were among the first NATO ground forces (KFOR) to enter Kosovo. The Glogovac region into which they deployed had been regarded as the heartland of the Kosovo Liberation Army; it had remained under Albanian control since the 1998 civil war.*

BELOW: *The arrival of KFOR soldiers in June 1999 turned Pristina into an armed camp virtually overnight. In the months since, the massive build-up of military logistics has only increased that image.*

(PHOTOS BY AUTHOR)

RIGHT: Twenty-five-year-old Peric Sladjan still has an AK-47 bullet lodged in his lower spine. While serving as a reservist in his home province of Kosovo, he was shot by his Albanian neighbour. He cannot be released from the Slankamen clinic until he has a home to go to.

BELOW: The flood of international aid has turned Pristina into a boom town. Convoys of trucks pour steadily into Kosovo and traffic congestion is becoming one of the major problems.

(PHOTOS BY AUTHOR)

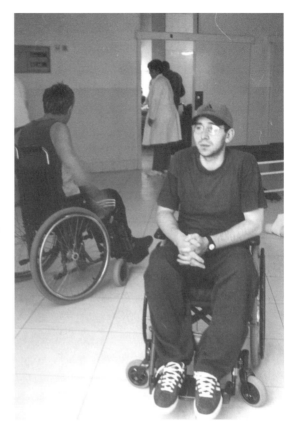

The actual numbers of revenge killings and abductions that have taken place since KFOR troops arrived in June remains in dispute. (Some sources claim more than 700 murders, and twice that many kidnappings, have occured during these six months.) However, everyone agrees that the level of violence is unacceptable.

"Yet, we are definitely making a difference," said Canadian Major Roland Lavie, a KFOR spokesman. "When NATO first arrived, there were about 36 murders a week. Now the average is only one a day."

KFOR estimates that only 97,100 Serbians still live in Kosovo. This represents roughly 50 per cent of the number calculated in a 1998 prewar census, and does not take into account some 100,000 refugees who sought refuge in Kosovo following their expulsion from Croatia and Bosnia.

On the other hand, nearly 80 per cent of the Albanians who were forced to flee from Kosovo have now returned to their homes. In just five months, they have created an incredible rebirth. Evidence of widespread vandalism in the city of Pristina has been almost eradicated. The influx of foreign aid workers, coupled with large-scale investment, has turned the Kosovo capital into something of a boom town. Still, essentials such as electricity and heating remain problematic.

However, city officials have promised to have the Pristina central heating plant functional by December 1, 1999. For its part, KFOR is concentrating on a major winterization program that will see at least one habitable room in every occupied dwelling in Kosovo. In Pristina, food staples remain plentiful, but transporting essentials into the more remote areas after the heavy snows start to fall remains a problem.

With the U.N. and KFOR relief effort gearing up to bring security to this region, random gunshots still echo nightly throughout the capital.

Pristina, November 27, 1999 (Saturday morning)   While trying to file my first story from Pristina I had a brief taste of the fear Kosovar Serbs live with daily. There were only two international phone lines out of the Grand Hotel, and both had to be accessed from the registration desk in the lobby. After being assigned one of the telephones, I had dialed the number of Vlada Kopric, my assistant/ translator in Belgrade. Since I did not possess a laptop computer, we had arranged to send copy from Kosovo via fax, then Vlada would forward it electronically to the *Ottawa Citizen*.

After entering just six of the ten required digits, I suddenly lost the dial tone.

An angry operator burst out of the switchboard office and loudly asked in English, "Why are you phoning Yugoslavia?" Before I could answer, he demanded, "Are you a Serb?" Immediately, the other patrons in the lobby fell silent, and several of the younger men began heading towards me. Thankfully, I was able to produce my recently-acquired KFOR press pass, and hastily blurt out that I was a Canadian journalist. Nevertheless, the operator persisted in questioning me.

The hotel manager was summoned and I was escorted into a private office. Away from the gathering crowd in the lobby, I was able to explain my situation.

Later that afternoon, I had a similar misadventure while trying to track down the Yugoslavian diplomatic mission in Pristina. I had been given contact names at the Foreign Affairs office in Belgrade, but no one could provide me with the exact office location. (Fearing Albanian attacks, the Yugoslavian diplomats were not about to hang a sign in front of their mission.) I therefore decided to enlist the aid of some of the international consulates which had set up shop in Kosovo. The Canadian representative proved useless, as he himself had yet to make contact with the Yugoslavian delegation.

I tried the Netherlands's mission next. The sole occupant of the tiny office was an Albanian translator. Initially, this young woman had been polite and helpful, but when she asked why I would wish to talk to these Serbs, I noticed a change in her demeanour. I acknowledged that both my current and wartime access into Kosovo had been authorized by the Yugoslav Army.

"So, you were here in Pristina before NATO arrived?" she asked, somewhat astonished.

"Just for the last couple of days," I explained.

"Well, what did you do to stop the killings?" she demanded.

When I stated that I had not actually seen any killings during my brief stay, her response was chilling. "You are a liar – *you* are a war criminal!"

I quickly left.

Last night, in Pristina, during the raucous Albanian flag day celebrations, four Serb civilians were dragged from their hiding places and beaten to death. While extremists may have been responsible for these brutal slayings, they were carried out in front of crowds of delighted, cheering Albanians.

Glogovac, Kosovo, November 27, 1999 (Saturday afternoon) There was no attempt to hide his pride in his men's performance as Captain Clint Austin related a dramatic incident that occurred last September.

As part of the Princess Patricia's Canadian Light Infantry Battle Group stationed in Kosovo, Austin's reconnaissance platoon had been tasked to enforce security at a Kosovo Liberation Army (KLA) funeral. One detachment, under the command of Sergeant Earl McCutcheon, had dismounted from their armoured vehicle in order to conduct weapon searches of the mourners. Around 10:00A.M., a sudden explosion rang out from behind nearby houses. Sergeant McCutcheon and his section raced to the scene to find a cluster of panicked civilians. One of the Albanian men yelled "Mina! Mina!" and pointed up a long grassy slope to where an elderly man lay prone. McCutcheon called in the situation report to headquarters and was advised that it would take at least 45 minutes to dispatch an ambulance to the scene.

Knowing the badly wounded old man would bleed to death before the ambulance got there, McCutcheon decided to risk his own life to save another's. Inch by cautious inch, he crept towards the injured victim, followed closely by Private Ross Weaver. They discovered that the Albanian farmer's right leg had been blown away below the knee; the rest of his body was bloody with shrapnel wounds. While Weaver administered a tourniquet and applied first aid, McCutcheon assisted in moving the man back down to the road where Captain Austin had hailed a passing Dutch Army medical team. With Canadian armoured vehicles providing an escort, they were able to reach the British field hospital in time for surgeons to save the Kosovar's life.

While both McCutcheon and Weaver have been recommended for (but not yet awarded) decorations for valour, their act of selflessness has already paid a dividend in terms of earning Canadians the trust and respect of the local citizens.

Since their arrival here in July, the Princess Pat's Battle Group has been instrumental in implementing the disarmament "Undertaking," signed between NATO and the Kosovo Liberation Army. "Our area of operations is located in the heartland of the KLA," said Lieutenant Colonel Shane Brennan, the Battle Group Commander. "Therefore it is crucial that we maintain a firm but fair approach to the weapons collection. The last thing we wanted to do was drive the KLA underground."

Under the terms of the NATO agreement, these former Albanian fighters are being offered three different career options. Most of them are being encouraged, with grants and scholarships, to resettle or retrain for a civilian profession. Some

5,000 have been recruited to constitute the new Kosovo Protection Corps, and a similar number are undergoing training to form the Kosovo Police Services.

The few Serbs remaining in the Canadian sector fear this development as they see it as nothing less than official recognition of the KLA – albeit with different names. The Canadians have made a concerted effort to allay these fears by demonstrating a strong measure of impartiality.

"Following a drive-by shooting and grenade attacks at one of our Serbian enclaves, we aggressively seized and detained the Albanians who were responsible," said Captain Wade Englesby, the second-in-command of Bravo Company. "Ever since, the Serbs have respected us. In fact, when we were ordered out of that particular sector, the inhabitants begged us to stay."

Bravo Company had a section of eight men stationed at the village of Radevo. Their mission was to prevent any revenge attacks against the 315 Serbian inhabitants.

Also within Bravo's task is a four-man permanent outpost to guard against vandalism at a nearby Orthodox church. In recent weeks, the Kosovo Protection Force has assembled a 188-man Rapid Response Guard comprised of the hardest core element of the former KLA. This unit has now taken up residence just a few kilometres from the Bravo Company camp. "We don't expect them to create any sort of havoc right here, in their own back yard," explained Englesby. "But the fear is that they'll be using it as a base from which to conduct acts of violence further afield."

The main threat to the safety of Canadian soldiers remains the vast amount of unexploded ordnance and booby traps that litter the Kosovo region, the most lethal of which are the cluster bomblets. Everything from an unexploded Tomahawk cruise missile to homemade hand grenades lies strewn about the ravaged hillsides.

It has been interesting for the Canadian soldiers to observe the impact and destructive power of the various munitions employed. NATO bombers seemed to have a penchant for destroying poultry farms. "We haven't yet figured out the military objective in obliterating all those chickens," said one soldier. "But it sure made one hell of a mess!"

As for tales of mortal combat between the KLA and Serb security forces, the lack of evidence has left most Canadians skeptical. "It was here in the Glogovac region that the KLA claim to have fought and won a major battle over a Serbian armoured column," said a Patricia captain. "Unfortunately, the telltale signs of such a conflict just aren't there. There are no shell craters, vehicle hulks or even spent (ammunition) casings. Nevertheless, the story has now become a legend."

With only days left to go in their tour of duty (at the time of my visit), the Princess Pats could be thankful that they've emerged relatively unscathed (the one exception being the tragic vehicle accident in which Sergeant Jerry Squires was killed). For veterans in the battle group, the drama which surrounded NATO's occupation of Kosovo has been replaced by an all-too-familiar routine. "If you take away the shootings, this tour is now just like Bosnia," stated one soldier.

Merdare, November 28, 1999 (Sunday morning)   There were only two buses a week from Kosovo into Serbia – on Monday and Friday. In order to catch my flight home from Budapest, I had to depart Pristina on Sunday. The only solution I could think of was to charter an Albanian taxi to the NATO/Yugoslavian border, and try to hitch a ride.

Not knowing how much Yugoslavia-bound traffic there would be on a Sunday morning, I left the Grand Hotel around 6:00A.M. Less than two hours later I arrived at the cluster of four parked Warriors (armoured personnel carriers) and grey bunker that constituted the British-manned checkpoint.

The morning was cold and damp, the sun having not yet fully risen, and the pair of British soldiers at the gate grumbled good-naturedly about the frigid weather.

Off to the left of the roadblock was a formidable-looking platoon bunker-cum-strongpoint. Barbed wire ringed the perimeter of this redoubt; the outer wall was constructed of shellproof, gravel-filled containers. A couple of sentries were evident in a guard tower, and two of the Warriors were manned, their engines running and turrets occasionally traversing the Serbian territory to their front.

The Brits informed me that the last civilian vehicle crossed their border post into Serbia 12 hours earlier. The odds of successfully catching a lift did not look good, so I decided to simply walk into Serbia. The two young corporals said they had no authority to stop me, and they weren't about to wake up their platoon commander and ask his permission.

According to these British infantrymen, quoting NATO intelligence as their source, the Yugoslavs were maintaining roving patrols along the border. These Serb special forces troops had reportedly set up a deadly array of booby traps and mines to prevent Albanians from crossing into their territory. These same elite MUPs (Yugoslav border police) had allegedly been halting cars just inside Serbia, and executing anyone suspected of being an ethnic Albanian.

The British troops felt they were providing the first line of defence against any large-scale Serbian attempt to reclaim Kosovo by force. "Our job here is to simply slow the Serbs up until our battalion can establish a blocking position across the main road, about a kilometre back," said one of the soldiers in a thick Scottish brogue. "For us, we expect it'll be a suicide mission."

Following such a dramatic situation report, my actual trek into Yugoslavia turned out to be laughably anticlimactic. The first Serbian checkpoint was about one-and-a-half kilometres from the British bunkers. As I walked down the middle of the road, I saw no evidence of any mines, boobytraps or bullet-riddled Albanian vehicles. As I approached the small portable trailer that marked Serbian territory, five middle-aged police officers came out to observe me. None of them was armed with anything more than a holstered pistol. There were no sandbags, no trenches and certainly no armoured vehicles. (The only means of transportation on hand was a blue and white Yugo automobile.) After a brief introduction in broken Serbian, my documents were seized by a sergeant, who promptly jumped into the little Yugo and sped off down the road. The four remaining police just shrugged their shoulders at this sudden departure, and said, "ne ma telefon" (no telephone). To prove their point, one of them pointedly showed me inside their trailer. I was astounded to see that it contained nothing but a camp cot.

Just inside Kosovo, nearly 1000 heavily armed British soldiers were dug in and mentally prepared for a massive Serbian onslaught. In reality, the so-called Yugoslav special forces, or elite MUPs, were so ill-equipped that reporting any incidents to their headquarters required a two-kilometre drive to the local groceteria pay phone.

◆ ◆ ◆ ◆ ◆ ◆ ◆ ◆ ◆ ◆

Zemun, Serbia, November 1999   In 1992, at the height of the conflict in Bosnia, over 100,000 Serbs took to the streets of Belgrade to protest Yugoslav President Slobodan Milosevic's handling of the war. To add to the political potency of this massive candlelight march, senior power company executive Jovan Mandic ordered his workers to black out the entire city. Immediately following the protest,

Yugoslavian national security police seized Mandic for interrogation.

During the next 48 hours, he was beaten in the basement of police headquarters, then released – without being charged with any offence.

If the message the Yugoslav security forces were trying to convey to Mandic was "Stop meddling in politics," they failed. During the three months of large-scale, daily demonstrations against Milosevic in 1996, Jovan Mandic resigned his power company post to add to the public protest. Since then, he has been dedicating his time and energy towards co-ordinating and organizing a viable opposition to the Milosevic regime. In a quiet Belgrade suburb, Mandic operates an underground club – a private bar catering to a select clientele of prominent Yugoslavs. Most Friday and Saturday nights, approximately 50 members of the Serbian intelligentsia – authors, musicians and actors – gather at Mandic's club to discuss politics, plot strategies and sing patriotic songs.

On the night of November 20, their discussions centered on the recent meeting of the Organization for European Security and Cooperation (OESC). While any formal participation at this conference by Milosevic's governing party had been rejected, leaders of Yugoslavia's federal opposition parties had been encouraged to attend. Vuk Draskovic, the controversial head of the Serbian Renewal Movement, had accepted the OESC's offer. By doing so, he incited the wrath of his government. "The traitor has gone to Istanbul to receive his new orders from NATO," was the official Yugoslav response.

Predictably, the reaction at the underground club was far more favourable. "The only way that our country can survive and rebuild is if we get help from the Western powers," said Jovan Mandic. "It is an important step that Draskovic has at least opened a dialogue with those who can bring us salvation." Among the patrons, there was a consensus that the Istanbul visit would ultimately benefit Yugoslavia, but there was little support for Vuk Draskovic himself. Since the massive protest rallies of 1996 fizzled out with a mutual pact between the Serbian Renewal Movement and Milosevic's government, few people trust Draskovic. "The marriage between Vuk and Slobo[dan] is a dirty one, and not something which will be easily forgotten," said Mr. Mandic.

Throughout Yugoslavia there is a small, but growing, wave of popular support for Zoran Djindic, the charismatic leader of the Democratic Party. At present, Djindic's main area of influence remains the central Serbian city of Nis. The regionalization and division of political parties has seriously hampered the collective opposition's attempts to capitalize on the public's dissatisfaction with the Milosevic regime. All of the major urban centres in Serbia – including Belgrade – are presently governed by representatives of the various opposition parties. In each of these cities the local officials exert direct influence over their various media outlets, who, in turn, send out political messages competing with RTS, the federal government's Radio and Television Service.

The result is that the majority of Serbs no longer trust the government, the opposition or the media. Unchannelled and unco-ordinated, public anger continues to be vented through public protests, albeit at ever-decreasing levels. The latest post-Kosovo conflict demonstrations reached their zenith in early October when 10,000 protestors in Belgrade had to be subdued by squads of riot police. By the end of November, the nightly marches were still being staged throughout Serbia, but few of these rallies attracted more than a few hundred participants.

"The people of Serbia have temporarily had their spirits broken," said Katarina Njegovan, a 22-year-old Belgrade University student. "They have been taking to the streets in the name of democracy for years – but to no avail." Njegovan, who first participated in a political rally at the age of 14, also believes that, at the moment, people are too preoccupied with simply surviving the winter. With the continuing trade sanctions crippling their economy and a transportation infrastructure in tatters following the NATO bombing campaign, there is a steadily mounting humanitarian crisis throughout Yugoslavia.

"By next fall, when the federal and republic elections are held, then the people will be ready to take to the streets once again to send their message to the [Milosevic] government," Njegovan predicted.

◆　◆　◆　◆　◆　◆　◆　◆　◆　◆

Pristina, Kosovo, November 1999　　In the autonomous region of Kosovo, the ethnic Albanian majority is preparing for upcoming elections in the spring of 2000. There are two main factions vying for control of what is seemingly destined to be an Independent Kosovo. The Kosovo Democratic League (LDK), headed by Ibrahim Rugova, has proven to be the more moderate party, while the Kosovo Liberation Army's political wing (UCK), led by Hashim Thaci, is increasingly regarded as a group of extreme ultra-nationalists. Both movements ultimately want to cut all ties with Yugoslavia, but they are also opposed to each other's divergent ideologies.

Immediately following the signing of the Kosovo peace agreement and the subsequent deployment of NATO troops, the UCK had been actively trying to solidify their control over the entire region. As refugees began flooding back to their ravaged homes, and foreign aid was poured into reconstruction projects, the former KLA began establishing an extensive network of local officials. "They would simply replace any of the LDK village headmen with their own people," said Captain Wade Englesby, an officer with the PPCLI Battle Group currently based out of Glogovac, Kosovo. "In this manner, the UCK have been effectively able to control the distribution of foreign aid to their own political advantage."

With the Kosovo elections scheduled for next spring, there has already been a marked heightening of tensions between supporters of the two Albanian political parties.

While revenge killings against Serbs and Gypsies still account for the bulk of the widespread violence in Kosovo, there is an ever-increasing level of politically-motivated inter-Albanian bloodshed being recorded by U.N./NATO authorities based in Pristina.

The UCK sees the upcoming elections as their best – and perhaps only – chance to seize power. Their desperation stems from the fact that the LDK's Ibrahim Rogova held a majority following among Kosovars prior to the NATO/Yugoslavia conflict.

Hashim Thaci's UCK realize it is imperative that their party capitalize quickly on the public euphoria created by the "KLA victory" over Serbian forces. In order to keep the nationalist fervour burning bright, Albanian schoolteachers are directed by UCK headmen to teach their pupils about the Serbian genocide of their people.

As a result, schoolchildren now regularly set up gauntlets to stone passing Serbian vehicles and buses. As NATO officials in Kosovo call for an end to such violence, and a "peaceful environment for all ethnicities," the circle of hate remains unbroken.

There are close to one million Serbian refugees (or displaced persons) currently living in congested camps such as the one in Pancevo *(RIGHT)*. Many of these individuals have been temporarily housed in these state facilities since being ethnically cleansed from Croatia in 1992 and 1995. It is estimated that over 100,000 Serbs have fled to these shelters from Kosovo since the arrival of NATO troops in June 1999.
Below, NATO maintains a Kosovo security force of 50,000 troops to prevent ethnic disputes and to quell the increasing inter-Albanian factional violence.
(*PHOTOS BY AUTHOR*)

ABOVE: *Canadian peacekeepers have been on constant deployment to the Former Yugoslavia since April 1992. With the Dayton Accord partition of Bosnia showing no signs of becoming a permanent solution, and ethnic violence still embroiling Kosovo, there appears to be no respite on the horizon. (PHOTOS BY AUTHOR)*

OPPOSITE PAGE: *While disputing the actual death toll of Yugoslavian civilians, NATO maintains that such killing of innocents was justifiable as an "act of humanity."*

9 - RESETTING THE STAGE

On Saturday, January 15, 2000, three Serbs, armed with automatic weapons, entered the lobby of the Belgrade International Hotel and unleashed a deadly fusillade. Their target, Zeljko Raznatovic – better known as "Arkan" – was killed instantly by three bullets, one of which pierced his right eye socket. Arkan's sister-in-law was badly wounded and one of his bodyguards also died.

In the wake of the brutal assassination, international media were awash in speculation about the killers and their motives. As a lifelong gangster and an indicted war criminal, Arkan had no shortage of enemies. Whatever the truth may be, a majority of Serbs have already passed judgement. They believe that Slobodan Milosevic orchestrated the hit on his former henchman. On February 8, Vlada Kopric sent an e-mail from Belgrade to *Esprit de Corps* magazine describing the fear and uncertainty gripping his country.

"As you've probably already heard, Arkan was killed only a few days after he sent his lawyers to The Hague Tribunal to negotiate his statement against Slobo. Now everyone here is expecting Arkan's sons – who are reputedly more ruthless than their father – to exact a measure of revenge. [On February 7] our Minister of Defence, Pavle Bulatovic, was also killed – and there's been no news about the incident ever since. We have a terrifying saying in Serbia, 'He was eaten by the dark.' Now this is an everyday occurrence."

In their reports on Arkan's funeral, the Western media focused primarily on the atrocities attributed to this ultra-nationalist Serbian warlord and on the lavish lifestyle he had lead.

What should not have gone unnoticed was the popular support Arkan's memory still commands, as evidenced by the large crowds of mourners. After nine consecutive years of bloody warfare, Serbian nationalism remains alive and unbowed.

After the Rambouillet peace plan went into effect and Yugoslavian troops began to withdraw from Kosovo, the Western media proclaimed victory over the Serbs. Beneath the jingoism and jubilant headlines, the truth was far more sobering. Throughout the hostilities, NATO's stated objective had been to drive Milosevic from office. As the war wound down, the Alliance said it did not wish to be a co-signatory to a peace plan with a "war criminal."

In the end NATO had been forced to negotiate with the Serb leader. Despite the massive 78-day air campaign, the presidency and powers of Slobodan Milosevic remained intact.

The second objective of NATO's air campaign had been the prevention of a humanitarian crisis in Kosovo. In fact, the bombing had triggered a Serbian offensive and a massive exodus of Albanians.

In a deft manoeuvre, NATO spin-doctors then proclaimed that their air attacks were now necessary to halt a humanitarian crisis. To justify escalating bombardments, NATO spoke of "genocide" and a death toll reaching 100,000.

When NATO forces finally deployed into Kosovo, the cost of their victory became apparent. Contrary to Jamie Shea's assertions, the Yugoslav Army had not been "seriously downgraded." As witnessed by the incoming NATO troops, the Serbs withdrew virtually intact. Since Kosovo remained sovereign Serbian territory, the positioning of NATO troops could hardly be called a "liberation." As for bringing peace and stability to Kosovo, that illusion was shattered when the KLA began a terror campaign of murder and looting against the Serb Kosovars. Hundreds of thousands of Serbs were forced from their homes.

Although the Albanian Kosovars had, with NATO's help, achieved their goal of throwing off the Serbian yoke, their colourful celebrations were premature. There remains the bitter internal fight for political control of an inevitably independent Kosovo. Extremists in the Albanian camp talk not only of "displacing" the remaining 90,000 Serbs, but of a "Greater Albania." This conceptual territory consists of approximately 90,000 square kilometres which, the hardliners say, historically belong to Albanians. At the moment, the landmass of Kosovo and Albania combined does not amount to 50,000 square kilometres. The fact that the remainder of "Greater Albania" lies in Macedonia, Greece, Serbia, Bosnia and Montenegro is not a deterrent.

Having failed to achieve any of their primary objectives, NATO desperately needed to validate their claims of Serbian genocide.

From the moment that NATO-led peacekeepers entered Kosovo, war crimes investigators were dispatched to dig up suspected mass gravesites.

When the first reports were released in November 1999, the forensic teams had probed 40 per cent of the sites. Only 670 bodies had been found. It was proof of ethnic hatred and local acts of terrorism, but it could not be labelled genocide or likened to the Holocaust. Spokespersons for the U.N. War Crimes Tribunal hastened to point out that there were still 60 per cent of the graves to be exhumed, but conceded that the largest and most likely sites had already been examined.

The Trepca mines had been one of the most reported-on sites of alleged genocide. Eyewitnesses in refugee camps had told Western reporters harrowing tales of Serbs bussing Albanians to the mine, slaughtering them and throwing their bodies down the shafts. It was said that these mine pits alone contained more than 700 corpses.

After an extensive search, the U.N. forensic team failed to find a single body. The largest mass grave, uncovered at Ljubenic, revealed only seven corpses – not the 350 initially reported.

When a Canadian journalist questioned Defence Minister Art Eggleton on the discrepancy between the U.N.'s body count and NATO's earlier claims, he had a ready response. With only a slight rewrite from the original air sortie retort prepared for General Henault, Eggleton looked the reporter in the eye and said sternly, "This is about human tragedy – it shouldn't be turned into a numbers game."

During the war, Eggleton's air force generals had been quick to point out the important role Canadian pilots played in the air campaign. With a bevy of charts and figures, these commanders had proudly demonstrated that Canada carried out ten per cent of the bombing sorties. However, when the numbers of Yugoslav civilian casualties caused by "illegitimate targeting" were released by the independent Human Rights Watch, no one in the Department of National Defence stepped forward to accept Canada's ten per cent of the responsibility.

By Yugoslavian estimates, our share of that responsibility would amount to 120 dead and 700 permanently disabled civilians. (The lower Human Rights Watch figures would still put Canada's bombing liabilities at 50 killed and 450 seriously injured civilians.) Apparently, what distinguishes NATO's killing and maiming of innocents from Serbian war crimes is that NATO acts in the name of humanity.

As the fog of war lifted, the Canadian Broadcast Corporation aired what amounted to a retraction of one of their Kosovar war stories. During the conflict, a CBC newsmagazine had produced a moving piece on a female guerrilla fighter. Through tears, the young Albanian had explained Serbs had raped and killed her younger sister. Forced to witness the atrocity, she had then enlisted in the KLA.

After the "liberation" of Kosovo, the CBC producer decided to do a follow-up on the young guerrilla fighter. When the television crew arrived, they were shocked to find the "dead" sister very much alive. Asked about the fabrication, the Albanians were unrepentant. "We did what we had to do. We could not beat the Serbs ourselves," they explained.

The CBC was able to admit that they had been tricked into broadcasting pro-Albanian propaganda. Unfortunately, the Canadian government had not been so willing to re-examine its own record on Kosovo. In the turbulent post-conflict period, Canada has continued to demonstrate an anti-Serb bias while simultaneously establishing closer ties with the Albanians. In November 1999, Foreign Affairs Minister Lloyd Axworthy made a visit to Pristina to open a Canadian diplomatic mission in the Kosovo capital.

Although Kosovo remains Serbian territory, Axworthy did not advise the Yugoslav authorities of his visit. The snub was compounded in January 2000, when Canada's former ambassador to Yugoslavia was turned away from our embassy in Belgrade on Axworthy's order. Since Ambassador James Bisset had been a vocal opponent of the NATO air attacks, Axworthy apparently thought the Serbs might use the visit for propaganda purposes. As it turned out, the Belgrade press had a field day with Canada's inability to tolerate divergent opinion.

One of the clearest examples of how little the Canadian government understands the complex Kosovo situations can be found in a letter Gerard Proteau received after he wrote to Jean Chrétien. It began: *"The Prime Minister has forwarded to me your e-mail message concerning "the increase of Albanian revenge killings in Kosovo." Canada has condemned the terrorist activities of the Kosovo Liberation Army, and the use of violence to achieve a political means. We have urged Kosovar leader Ibrahim Rugova to*

denounce terrorism and the use of force in the struggle for greater autonomy for Kosovo...."
The letter, dated October 22, 1999, was signed by Lloyd Axworthy.

From the outset, Rugova has been the moderate, pacifist voice of the Albanian Kosovar movement. He is vehemently opposed to KLA terrorism and violence. During the bombing campaign, NATO erroneously claimed (and never renounced) that Milosevic had executed him. Hashim Thaci, the leader of the militant KLA faction known as UCK, has pronounced Rugova a traitor and has put him on the list of enemies. Canadian soldiers on patrol in Kosovo are fully aware of the bitter and often violent dispute between Rugova's Democratic League and the UCK. Even the name of the KLA had been changed to the Kosovo Protection Corps (KPC), as the KLA, in theory, had been disbanded and disarmed.

Although we have 1200 soldiers on the ground and a diplomatic mission in Pristina, our political leaders appear to be dangerously ignorant of the major players in the Balkan crisis.

The person Axworthy and Chrétien should be dealing with on the subject of Kosovar violence is none other than the new KPC commander, the infamous Medak-Krajina war criminal, General Agim Ceku.

LEFT: *Despite the presence of 50,000 NATO peacekeepers, violence and terrorism remain rampant in Kosovo. Revenge attacks against the few remaining Serbs are perpetrated by former KLA fighters. It is their objective to ethnically cleanse the province prior to the projected 2002 referendum on indpendence. In addition, there has been a marked increase in inter-Albanian factional strife as the two major movements – Rugova's LDK and Thaci's UCK – battle for control of postwar Kosovo. By February 2000, continued instability prompted NATO officials to talk of bolstering their already sizeable military presence in the region. (AP)*

This map constitutes the "Greater Albania" concept which the extremists among the Kosovar fighters still believe they are striving for. It was drawn by Albanian Political Emigration *and first published in the book* Kosovo Origins, *by Hugo Roth. This 90,000-square-kilometre region incorporates land currently recognized as Greece, Macedonia, Bosnia, Serbia and Montenegro.*

SLOBODAN MILOSEVIC

President of Yugoslavia. It was in 1987 that "Slobo" first revived the spirit of Prince Lazar to ignite Serbian nationalism. Despite eight years of bloody civil war, the NATO air campaign, devastating losses and a shattered economy, Serbian pride remains unbroken. And Milosevic remains the President. (RTS)

HASHIM THACI

Leader of the UCK (Kosovo Liberation Army). The 39-year-old Albanian Kosovar is viewed as a violent extremist. His policies regarding the future of Kosovo go beyond an independent state which contains a Serb minority; his fighters are committed to an ethnically 'pure' Greater Albania. (PHOTO COURTESY AGENCE FRANCE)

IBRAHIM RUGOVA

Leader of the Democratic League of Kosovo (LDK). This academic is regarded as the pacifist-moderate voice of the Albanian Kosovars. While Milosevic continued to negotiate with him, the KLA denounced him as a traitor – and NATO pronounced him dead. Lloyd Axworthy apparently isn't familiar with his political stance. (REUTERS)

KOSOVO CONFLICT: THE PLAYERS AND EVENTS

APRIL 1996 - A secretive group, the Kosovo Liberation Army (KLA) claims responsibility for the murder of Serb civilians and policemen in the Decan and Pec regions of southern Kosovo in a letter to the BBC World Service. The letter is dismissed as a Serb plot to clamp down in Kosovo.

NOVEMBER 29, 1997 - KLA publicly reveals itself for the first time at the funeral of an Albanian teacher shot to death by Serb security forces. Three masked, armed and uniformed members of the KLA appear before an appreciative crowd of 20,000 mourners.

FEBRUARY 1998 - After several attacks on policemen, Yugoslav President Slobodan Milosevic sends thousands of Serb police and special forces into Kosovo, supported by armoured personnel carriers.

MARCH 5 - Serb forces launch a major assault west of Pristina, the provincial capital of Kosovo, killing 26 KLA fighters. Similar offensives in the Drenica region leave 5000 homeless.

MARCH 9 - Six-member Contact Group (United States, Britain, France, Italy, Germany and Russia) imposes additional economic and diplomatic sanctions against Serbia. Consensus shaky at best and fighting escalates as arms are smuggled across the border from Albania.

APRIL 25 - U.S. President Bill Clinton threatens additional sanctions if Belgrade does not open talks with Albanian Kosovar leader Ibrahim Rugova, a moderate often at odds with Muslim firebrands and the KLA. Milosevic invites Rugova to a meeting in Pristina brokered by U.S. special envoy Richard Holbrooke.

MAY 25 - Referendum in Serbia: 95 per cent agree with Milosevic that Kosovo is an internal problem and international intervention should not be allowed.

MAY 27 - Rugova travels to Washington to warn Clinton that Kosovo is sliding into a general war. Clinton, deeply distracted by the Lewinsky affair, promises him that the province will not become another Bosnia.

MAY 31 - Serbs open offensive to clear KLA from border areas. Some 10,000 made homeless, and 50,000 refugees flee to Albania, Macedonia and Montenegro. General Wesley Clark, Supreme Commander of NATO forces in Europe, confirms that he is looking at "detailed studies of possible preventive deployment" on the Albanian border. NATO commissions Operation *Determined Falcon* – mock bombing raids by aircraft based in Aviano, Italy.

AUGUST 4 - After assuring

JAMIE SHEA

NATO spokesman. Regarded by the Albanians as the "true liberator" of Kosovo. Shea manipulated the truth throughout the entire air campaign. An aggressive orator, Shea was the most prominent television personality (worldwide) during the conflict. His unrepentant jingoistic hatred for the Serbs helped to "dehumanize the enemy." (AP)

MADELEINE ALBRIGHT

U.S. Secretary of State. During the Rambouillet peace talks, Albright's actions made it very clear that NATO – and in particular the U.S. – were bent on forcing a resolution through bombing. The Albanians had only conceded to sign the deal after learning that without their signature, NATO would not bomb Yugoslavia. Her will prevailed. (AFP)

JEAN CHRÉTIEN

Prime Minister of Canada. From the outset, Canada allowed the U.S. State Department to dictate our foreign policy on Kosovo. Our overtasked military provided strike aircraft and peacekeepers to uphold our stakeholding as a partner in NATO. However, Canada – and Chrétien – were invisible on the world stage.

(PHOTO TOM HANSON, CP)

European Union representatives that the "skirmish" was over, Milosevic launches a major counter-offensive encircling the KLA in central Kosovo. An additional 70,000 refugees flee the province.

SEPTEMBER 23 - U.N. Security Council passes Resolution 1199, China abstaining, calling for all parties to cease hostilities. Fighting intensifies and the number of refugees climbs to 300,000. Holbrook and Milosevic meet in Belgrade.

OCTOBER 12 - NATO announces Operation *Deliberate Force*, giving military commanders the authority to launch limited airstrikes. Milosevic pledges compliance with Resolution 1199, allowing up to 2000 verifiers, including Canadians, into Kosovo under the supervision of the Organization for Security and Cooperation in Europe. KLA states that "all solutions but independence are not

acceptable." Firefights continued.

OCTOBER 22 - U.S. Ambassador Christopher Hill holds meetings with Rugova and representatives of the KLA in Prisitina to work on the draft of a political agreement and to quicken the pace of negotiations. Yugoslav troops return to barracks and NATO leaders confirm that Milosevic had fulfilled his part of the bargain. OSCE monitors enter Kosovo on November 7. KLA regroups and touts itself as the sole legitimate representative of the Albanian Kosovars.

DECEMBER 16 - Milosevic criticizes U.S. for refusing to label the KLA "a terrorist organization." Clashes escalate during the winter. In his New Year's address to the nation, Milosevic vows to resist with force any bid to separate Kosovo from Serbia. Rugova calls for U.N. peacekeepers.

JANUARY 16, 1999 - Massacre

of civilians at Racak inflames international opinion. U.S. threatens military action against the Serbs. Representatives from all sides summoned to Rambouillet, near Paris, to work out an accord along the lines of the U.S.-backed three-year interim autonomy agreement, with a referendum to be held later. Serbs complain of "being marched at gunpoint to Rambouillet" by an "obviously biased NATO."

FEBRUARY 6 - Talks begin at Rambouillet with the Serbs submitting a plan to restore autonomy to Kosovo on condition that no foreign troops enter the province. The plan is rejected by U.S. Secretary of State Madeleine Albright. Talks teeter on the brink of collapse and fighting continues as NATO renews the threat of airstrikes.

MARCH 18 - Albanian Kosovars sign the Rambouillet Accord in a ceremony at the Arc de Triomphe

VIKTOR CHERNOMYRDIN

Russian special envoy. It was the tireless efforts and endless bouts of shuttle diplomacy by Chernomyrdin that finally brought about the shaky Kosovo peace deal. On two occasions (the bombing of the Chinese Embassy and the indictment of Slobodan Milosevic), ill-timed NATO actions served to prolong the peace process.

BILL CLINTON

U.S. President. For Clinton, the media distraction caused by the Kosovo conflict was a welcome relief. In the preceding months he had been embroiled in the Monica Lewinsky sex scandal; he still faced impeachment hearings and perjury charges. Clinton denounced the January 16 Racak massacre, and set the wheels of NATO intervention in motion.

LOUISE ARBOUR

Chief Prosecutor, U.N. War Crimes Tribunal. This Canadian judge was the driving force behind the May 27, 1999, indictment of Slobodan Milosevic as a war criminal. Following the Yugoslav Army's withdrawal from Kosovo in June, forensic teams scoured suspected mass gravesites for evidence to substantiate the charges. (PHOTO AMEL EMRIC, AP)

boycotted by the Serbs. Belgrade braces for war.

MARCH 24 - Bombing begins. General Clark states: "We are going to systematically and progressively attack, disrupt, degrade, devastate, and ultimately destroy Yugoslav forces and their facilities and support." Over 400 aircraft strike targets througout Serbia.

MARCH 25 - Stealth fighters join the air campaign as Belgrade orders Western media out of Kosovo and continues attacks on Albanian Kosovars. Number of refugees and internally displaced reaches 900,000.

MARCH 27 - A U.S. F-117 Nighthawk Stealth fighter is shot down near Belgrade.

MARCH 31 - Three U.S. soldiers are captured by Serb forces on the Macedonian border. Russia sends warships into the Adriatic and

Canada commits six more CF-18 fighters to its force in Aviano.

APRIL 1 - NATO warplanes destroy first of three bridges over the Danube at Novi Sad. Ethnic cleansing continues in Kosovo and western leaders accuse Milosevic of "genocide." Canada offers to take in 5000 refugees.

APRIL 13 - Belgrade reports ten dead and 18 injured on a train hit by a NATO missile. Operation *Allied Harbour* launched, deploying 10,000 troops to support humanitarian relief to refugees in countries neighbouring Kosovo.

APRIL 15 - NATO admits one of its warplanes hit a civilian convoy in southwest Kosovo killing 73.

APRIL 20 - Twenty-four U.S. Apache AH-64 attack helicopters arrive in Albania.

APRIL 22 - NATO raids destroy Milosevic's official Belgrade

residence. Two days later Radio Belgrade is knocked off the air.

MAY 1 - Forty-seven bus passengers are killed when NATO bombs a bridge in Kosovo.

MAY 3 - Russian special envoy Victor Chernomyrdin arrives in Washington for talks. NATO blacks out most of Serbia with a new "soft bomb," short-circuiting power equipment. "We have our finger on the light switch now," says NATO spokesman Jamie Shea.

MAY 5 - First 300 Kosovar refugees arrive at CFB Trenton.

MAY 8 - NATO missiles hit the Chinese Embassy killing three people. Thousands of Chinese protest in Beijing, stoning the U.S. Embassy. NATO describes the bombing as "a tragic mistake" caused by "faulty information." Military and political analysts claim that NATO has "taken a disaster and turned it into a catastrophe."

ZELJKO 'ARKAN' RAZNATOVIC
Serbian paramilitary commander. From his early career as a bank-robber, Arkan seized the violent opportunity presented by the break-up of Yugoslavia to elevate himself to notorious warlord. His volunteer Tigers were among the most ruthless of the units that fought in Croatia and Bosnia. He was gunned down in Belgrade on January 14, 2000. (REUTERS)

LLOYD AXWORTHY
Minister of Foreign Affairs (Canada). In an October 22, 1999, letter to one of his constituents, Axworthy revealed his rudimentary understanding of who the primary players were in the Kosovo conflict. Canadian soldiers were on the front lines, but the man who sent them there couldn't accurately explain why. (DND PHOTO)

ARTHUR EGGLETON
Minister of Defence (Canada). On April 7, 1999, when NATO leaders first agreed to commit ground forces into Kosovo without a prior peace deal, Eggleton errantly let the cat out of the bag. The Pentagon issued a categorical denial, but the damage was done. For the remainder of the campaign, Eggleton was virtually silenced. (DND PHOTO)

MAY 14 - Belgrade claims that 79 people were killed and 58 wounded when missiles hit the southern Kosovo village of Korisa. NATO says it was a legitimate target as it housed a Serb military command post.

MAY 25 - NATO military experts propose boosting the number of troops in a Kosovo Force to 50,000.

MAY 27 - Justice Louise Arbour, of the International War Crimes Tribunal, announces indictments against Yugoslav President Slobodan Milosevic and four others for crimes against humanity, holding them responsible for atrocities in Kosovo and the expulsion of the Albanian minority. It is the first time an international court has charged a sitting head of state with war crimes.

MAY 28 - EU representative, Finnish President Martti Ahtisaari, U.S. Deputy Secretary of State, Strobe Talbot, and Russian envoy,

Victor Chernomyrdin, meet in Moscow. Chernomyrdin leaves for Belgrade the next day and insists that the NATO bombing must end as a condition for meaningful talks.

MAY 29 - NATO bombs knock out the entire Serbian power system.

MAY 31 - At least 11 were killed and 40 wounded in an attack on a bridge in Varvarin, in central Serbia. Seven more bodies are dug out of the rubble of Istok prison which was razed by NATO airstrikes on May 19 and 21, bringing the death toll to 93.

JUNE 2 - Ahtisaari, Chernomyrdin and Talbot meet in Bonn and announce that efforts to end the Yugoslav crisis are at a decisive stage. KLA launches offensive backed by NATO air power.

JUNE 3 - Talks resume in Belgrade. Yugoslav government accepts peace proposals. Bombing continues.

JUNE 4 - Ahtisaari reports to EU that Yugoslavia has agreed to a military pullout from Kosovo, and to the deployment of an international force (KFOR). Under the auspices of the U.N., Kosovar citizens would enjoy "substantial autonomy." Canada commits 800 troops from Lord Strathcona's Horse and 408 Tactical Helicopter Squadron.

JUNE 6 - Yugoslav Army delegation and U.N. representatives meet in the northern Macedonian town of Kumanovo.

JUNE 10 - Agreement reached at Kumanovo. Bombing ends. Thousands of war-weary Serbs celebrate in the streets of Belgrade.

JUNE 12 - Serb forces begin to leave Kosovo as Russian troops occupy Slatina airport in Pristina and 5000 NATO peacekeepers fan out across the province.
Compiled by Dr. B. Twatio.

INDEX

Ahtisaari, Martti: 75, 76, 90
Albanians
    future goals: 144
        Greater Albania: *148*
    refugee convoy bombed: *40*
Albright, Madeleine: 16, 38, 61, *150*
    manipulates start of bombing: 31
    meets with Albanians: 31
    works on peace proposal: 44
Arbour, Louise: 30, *151*
    announces war crimes indictments: 61
Arkan. *See Raznatovic, Zeljko*
Austin, Captain Clint: 133
Axworthy, Foreign Affairs Minister Lloyd: *152*
    opens diplomatic mission in Kosovo: 146
Battle of Kosovo
    second, 1448: 22
Battle of Skopje: 23
    Great Migration: *21*
Belgrade: 50, 52, 59, 60, 62, 63, 64,
        67, 68, 72, 75, 76, 77, 79, 86,
        88, 89, 119
    attacks on: 75
    bomb kills two children: 61
        funeral of: 63 -64
    bombing initiated: 31
    cruise missile hits: 79
    estimated bomb damage to: 78
    foreign journalists ousted from: 34
    military hospital: *84*
    police: 120
    work camp: 81 -82
Berisja, Sala: 81, *84*
Bezanija cemetery: 63
Black market: 51
    contraband: 52
    fuel: 51, 119
    money supply: 54
Brankovic, Djurad: 22
Brankovic, Vuc: 22
Brennan, Lieutenant Colonel Shane: 134
British Army
    5th Parachute Brigade: 98
        presence in Pristina: 106
    arrive at Pristina airport: 100
    troops move toward Pristina: 98
Bucaj, Sylejman: 100 -102

    daughter attacked: 102
    return to Pristina: 102
Bugarcic, Bojan: 34, 123 -124
    admits to use of propaganda: 124
    comments on peace deal: 123 -124
    comments on Yugoslav Air Defence: 124
Calvin, Lieutenant Colonel Jim: 13
    briefs Parliament on Medak Pocket: 14
Canadian Broadcast Corporation
    retracts story: 146
Canadian Embassy
    vandalized: 52, *53*
Carter, President Jimmy: 37
Ceku, General Agim: 15, *19*, 147
    Medak Pocket: 14
    takes command of KLA: 19
Chernomyrdin, Viktor: 44, 75, 76, *151*
    peace plan collapses: 44
    visits to Belgrade: 77
Chinese Embassy
    bombed: 44, *91*
Chomic, Gordana: 122
Chrétien, Prime Minister Jean: 41, 146, 147,
    150
Clark, General Wesley: 42
Clark, Tom: 43
Clinton, President Bill: 12, 16, *151*
    airstrikes launched: 16
    outrage over discovery at Racak: 30
    reacts to capture of three U.S. marines: 38
Conference of the Ambassadors: 24
Congress of Berlin: 23
CTV. *See Clark, Tom*; *MacKenzie, Major*
    General Lewis
Danube River: 72
    ferry system: *53*, 56
    pontoon bridge: 121
Davis, Jim: 16
Dayton Peace Accord: 28
Djindic, Zoran: 138
Dragas, Mirjana: 71
Dragasevich, Bora: 48
Draskovic, Vuk: 138
Dunn, Sergeant Colin: 127
Economic sanctions: 52
Eggleton, Defence Minister Art: 41, *152*
    discusses discrepancies: 145

Englesby, Captain Wade: 135, 140
Esprit de Corps: 12, 143
Ethell, Colonel Don
    criticizes airstrikes: 18
Federal Republic of Yugoslavia
    committee for co-operation: 127
Federation of Yugoslav Republics: 25
Ferdinand, Archduke Franz
    assassination of: 24
Forand, Major General Allain: 15
Garvey, Bruce: 50
Genocide
    Ljubenic: 145
    NATO's claims of: 145
    Trepca mines: 145
Glogovac: 133, 135
Goshi, Bahri: 106
Grdelica
    train bombed: *39*
Great Migration: 23
Hague War Crimes Tribunal, The. *See* United
        Nations
Henault, Lieutenant General Ray: 42
Hitler, Adolph
    invades Yugoslavia, 1941: 25
Holbrooke, Ambassador Richard: 34
Hoppe, Sergeant Tom: 17
    decorated for bravery: 17
Horner, Nils: 100, 106
Hotels
    Blue: 118
    Grand: 100, 108, 136
        conditions in: 109
    Hyatt: 54, 59
    Moskva: 11, *57*, 59, 67, 70, 79
        return to: 112, 118
    World War Two: *27*
House, Danielle: *59*
Hrebeljanovic, Prince Lazar: 22
Hrnic, Rade: 106
Ilic, Mladen: *83*
Information front
    NATO control of: 114
Isteric, Slavisa. *See Kosovo Liberation Army
    (KLA): Slavisa Isteric killed*
Ivkovac, Aleksander: 121
Jackson, Lieutenant General Michael: 45, 80, 86
Jackson, Reverend Jesse
    secures release of US servicemen: 44
Jashari, Adem

KLA commander
    killed: 29
Jovic, Petra: 95
Jukic, Vesna: 98, 108
Kachak
    replaced by KLA: 28
    separatist movement: 25
Karadzic, Radovan: 37
KFOR
    Russian troops arrive: 108
Kodra-E-Trimave: 102
Kopric, Andjelka: 33
Kopric, Radmilla: 49
Kopric, Vlada: 49, 67, 132, 143
    credentials confiscated: 72 -73
    fooled by propaganda: 124
Kopric, Zlatan: 21, 49
Kosovo: 12, 18
    conditions in: 94
    convoy into: 93 -96
    elections: 139
    escalating unrest: 29
    first wave of Catholic Albanians arrive, 1448: 22
    police vehicles withdraw: *115*
    resettlement program initiated: 29
    security force: *141*
    separatist riots: 26
    Serbian residents: *128*, 132
    Serbs return to: 127
    Yugoslav army withdraws: *103*
Kosovo Democratic League (LDK): 35, 139
Kosovo Liberation Army (KLA): 19
    attacks intensify: 82, 87
    attacks on main auto-route: 99
    born: 28
    bus ambush: 87
    career options: 134
    changes identity: 147
    control of Prellez: 102
    emboldened: 106
    funeral: 134
    ground offensives: 78
    opens Pristina headquarters: 106
    Red Patch unit: 106
    Slavisa Isteric killed: 106 -107
    terror campaign: 144
Kosovo Liberation Army (UCK): 139
Kosovo Police Services: 134
Kosovo *polje*: 22
    invasion force, 1389: 22

Milosevic dispatched to: 26
Milosevic's address to: 28
Kosovo Protection Corps (KPC): 134, 147
   Rapid Response Guard: 135
Krajina: 15, *20*, 48
Krusevac: 110
Krusik factory
   bombed: 70
Kursumliga: 111
Lavie, Major Roland: 132
Lazar, Prince Hrebelyanovic: 22
   battle of Kosovo polje: 22
Leslie, Colonel Andrew: 15
Lewinsky, Monica: 30
Lockhart, Joe: 37
Lord Strathcona's Horse (LdSH)
   firefight outside Visoko: 17
   Kosovo patrol: 127
Macedonia
   peace talks end: 80
   refugee camps: 108
   withdrawal talks begin: 79
MacKenzie, Major General Lewis: *19*, 36, 43
   criticizes airstrikes: 18
   discounts polling: 38
Mandic, Jovan: 120, 137
Marijanovic, Colonel General Sueterav: 86
Martineau, Warrant Officer Tom: 17
Matanovic, Nada: 126, *129*
Matic, Goran: 61, 77
Matic, Zeljko: 72
McCutcheon, Sergeant Earl: 134
McNaughton, Derek: 50
Medak Pocket: 13
Merdare: 136
Mianjovic, Milan: 125
Michitsch, Howard: 16
Mihailovic. *See Royalist Chetniks*
Mihailovic, Dragoljub: 25
Milosevic, Slobodan: 34, 54, 64, 76, 137,
     144, *149*
   agrees to peace terms, 1995: 36
   concedes to UN demands: 29
   conditions of signing: 90
   Deputy President of: 26
     speaks at Kosovo polje: 26 -28
   elected President: 28
     policies protested: 28
   indicted for war crimes: 60
   'murders' Ibrahim Rugova: 36

   protests against: 119
   signs initial peace proposal: 44
Mussolini, Benito: 25
NATO
   accredited journalist: 108
   air campaign's civilian death toll: 126
   air raids: 80
   Alliance: 12
   bombs refugee convoy: *40*
   claims of victory: 144
   daylight raids: 79
   discrepancy in claims: 100
   ground operation initiated: 44
   impact on violence: 132
   intensifies air campaign: 80
   KFOR: 98
   KFOR checkpoint: 127
   Lord Strathcona's Horse: 127
   objectives: 144
   peacekeeping force
     Canada's commitment to: *128*, *130*
   targets Yugoslav Foreign Ministry: 123
   television networks bombed: *39*
   troops arrive in Pristina: 97, *104*
Nazis: 33
   Belgrade executions: *27*
   recruit Croats: 25
Nebojosa, Vujovic: 82
New Belgrade: 50, 59
Nis: 93, 138
   tobacco factory bombed: 42 -43
Njegovan, Katarina: 33, 139
Novi Sad: 48, 55, 55 -56
   bridges destroyed: *117*
   destruction of bridge: *66*
   destruction of bridges: 121
   ferry system: 121
   first snowfall: 121
   housing complex bombed: *46*
   oil refinery: 55
   reconstruction of bridges: 121 -122
   unemployment high: 122
Obrenevac
   power plant: 75
Obrenevic, Prince Milan: 23
Opacic, Branko: 69
Opacic, Pavle: 121
Operation
   Deliberate Force: 36
   Storm: 14, 15

Organization for European Security and Co-
operatio: 138
Ottawa *Citizen*: 50
Ottoman: 22
conquest of Serbia, 1459: 22
Pancevo
bridge to: 55
oil refinery hit: 81
refugee camp: *83*
Pavlovic family
funeral of children: 63
funeral of Dijana: *58*
Peace deal
Albanians sign: 31
bogged down: 75
celebration of: 88
ended: 80
explanation of: 86
initial schedule: 78
June 3rd signing of: *74*
reasons for impasse: 89
Russians and Ottomans: 23
signed: 88
Yugoslav Parliament votes on: 77
Peacekeeping force
composition of: 77
Popovic, Ljiljana: *116*
death of son, Sasha: 122
Popovic, Sasha: *116*
death of: 123
Power outage: 59, 62, 67, 79, *83*
Princess Patricia's Canadian Light Infantry (PPCLI:
134, 140
Bravo Company: 135
heroic actions: 134
Second Battalion
Medak Pocket: 13
successfully implement disarmament agree-
ment: 134
threat to: 135
Princip, Gavrilo: 24
Pristina: 96, 98, 132, 139
Albanian revenge gauntlet
British soldiers monitor: *104*
arrival of KFOR soldiers: *130*
boom town: *131*
buildings torched: *92*
reporters secreted into: 93
Prizren: 87
Prizren League: 23

Propaganda: *57*, 61, 124
surrounding end of peace talks: 82 -86
Public Affairs branch
spins results of airstrikes: 41 -42
Pugliese, David: 14
Racak: 30
Radical Party. *See Seselj, Vojisalv*
Radio-Television Serbia (RTS): 139
bombed: 43
Rambouillet: 30, 34
Accord: 41
talks break down: 35
Treaty: 31
Serbian objections to: 31
Raznatovic, Zeljko: 64 -67, *152*
death of: 143
funeral of: 144
Red Cross: 71
Refugees
Albanians claim atrocities: 38
Albanians into Macedonia: 36
Reinhart, General Klaus: 127
Republike Square: 89
concert: 80
rock concert: *66*, *91*
Serbian folk dancers: *84*
Revenge killings: 127
Royal 22nd Regiment (Vandoos): 14
Royalist Chetniks: 25
Rugova, Ibrahim: 30, 35 -36, 139, 147, *149*.
See also Kosovo Democratic League (LDK)
Russia
troops arrive in Kosovo: 97
Russo-Ottoman war: 23
Sarajevo: 36
market bombed: 16
playground shelled: 16
Sava River: 59
Seipagarvi, Irmeli: 94, 100
Serbia
air defence downs Stealth bomber: 35
black humour: 62
buses damaged: *105*
communist guerrillas: 25
cost of war: 89
families flee Pristina: *93*
folk dancers: *84*
following attacks: 144
invasion of: 24
military alliance, 1912: 24

military and refugees flee, 1915: **27**
Orthodox religion: 63
Pancevo refugee camp: **141**
police: 99
policeman, Tequila: 99
public protests: 118
re-captures Kosovo: 24
reaction to first bombing: 34
refugees: **20**
refugees flee KLA violence: 144
refugees flee Kosovo: 96 -97, **103**, **115**
residents of Kosovo: 132
retreat, 1915: 24
Special Forces: 136
spirit: 119
    broken: 139
tractor convoys: **105**
Treaty of Versailles signed: 24 -25
vandalization of embassies: 34
vital resources destroyed
    humanitarian crisis imminent: 119
withdrawal from Kosovo: 87
withdrawal from Pristina: 96
Serbian National Shield Society of Canada: 48
Serbian Renewal Movement: 138
Seselj, Vojisalv:
    breaks ranks with Serbian parliament: 90
Sharp End, The: A Canadian Soldier's Story. *See*
    Davis, Jim
Shea, Jamie: 34, 43, 98, 100, **150**
    announces Rugova's 'murder': 35
    cheered as hero: 113
    claims criminals sent to front lines: 35
    reacts to train bombing: 42
    spins surrender of US marines: 37
Simic, Slavoljub: 70
Skenderberg SS: 25
Skilliter, Trooper Jason: 17
    decorated for bravery: 17
Sladjan, Peric: 125, **131**
Slankamen: 124
    neurological clinic: 124 -127, **129**
Squires, Sergeant Jerry: 136
Srebrenica: 16
Stalin, Joseph: 26
Stopford, Warrant Officer Matt: **19**
    criticizes NATO: 18
    honoured for Medak Pocket: 14
Subotica: 47
Surdilica

sanatorium bombed: 113 -114
Tadic, Dr. Radenko: 125
Talbott, Strobe: 75
Tasic, Natasha: 43
Tesic, Dragoljub: **65**, 70
Thaci, Hashim: 30, 35, 139, 140, 147, **149**.
    See also Kosovo Liberation Army (UCK)
Tito, Marshal Josip: 25, 26, 49. *See also*
    Serbia: communist guerrillas
    establishes control of Federation of Yugoslav
    Rep: 25
    forces Germans out of Kosovo: 25
    gives autonomy to Kosovo: 26
Trade sanctions
    effect of: 51
Treaty of Trianon: 24
Tudjman, President Franjo: 15
Turkish Empire
    challenge to, 1690: 23
Turks
    ethnic cleansing, 1737: 23
United Nations
    Hague War Crimes Tribunal, The: 60
        announcement of war: 77
    Security Council: 29
        ceasefire demanded: 29
        Resolution 1199: 29
    Verification Force: 30
    War Crimes Tribunal: 15, 30
        reference mass graves: 145
Ustasha SS: 25
Valjevo: 70
    hospital: 70 -71
Velickovic, Colonel: 73, 93
Vendors: **65**, **74**
Vesti: 49
Visoko: 17
Vojvadina: 117
Vukovic, Radmila: 80
Weaponry/Armament
    Aircraft
        CF-18 fighter jets: **32**
        F-117 Nighthawk Stealth: 35
        MiG 29 fighter aircraft: 100
        B-52 bomber: 87
    Anti-aircraft
        23 mm air defence guns (Yugoslav): **104**
        artillery (AAA): 96
        SA-6 missiles: 51
    Missiles

surface-to-air (SAM): 96
Tomahawk: 43, 44, 67, 81
Vehicles
 Bison APC: **45**
 T-64 tanks: 111
 T-72 tanks: 111
 Warrior APC: 136
Weapons
 AK-47 assault rifle: 70
 cluster bombs: 126, 135
 smart bombs: 38, 41, 124
Weaver, Private Ross: 134
World War One
 armistice signed: 24
 starts: 24
Writer's Club: 64 -67
Yugo Import Building: 78

unexploded missile lands in: 67 -68
Yugoslav Army
 Press Centre: 50, 75
 soldiers of: 69
 withdraws from Pristina: 96
Yugoslavia
 costs skyrocket: 119
 Foreign Ministry
  targetted: 123
 medical facilities: 71 -72
 MUPs (border police): 136
 return to: 117
 Treasury bankrupt: 119
Zelko, Micic: 125, 129
Zemun: 11, 137
 anti-aircraft fire: 81
 transformers bombed: **47**, 75

1) The Serbian armoured forces in Kosovo were equipped with T-72 main battle tanks, which proved to be elusive targets for the NATO aircraft. After 78 days of bombing, only 13 Serb tanks were destroyed – mostly by KLA landmines.
2) U.S. B-52 heavy bombers were employed in the latter stages of the conflict. As KLA guerrillas forced Serb militia units into the open, B-52s pulverized the Serbs with massive payloads of cluster bombs. 3) NATO's sophisticated HARM (Highspeed Anti-Radar) missiles were used to deadly effect during the initial airstrikes. As soon as the Yugoslav air defences turned on their radars, they would be destroyed. 4) Yugoslavian-built SA-6 surface-to-air missile launchers provided the only real (albeit remote) threat to NATO fighters. Unable to utilize their radars, Serbs resorted to firing their SA-6s "blind." 5) Sophisticated, U.S. ship-launched Tomahawks – in conjunction with air-dropped cruise missiles – provided the mainstay of NATO's guided projectile bombardment. (U.S. D.O.D)

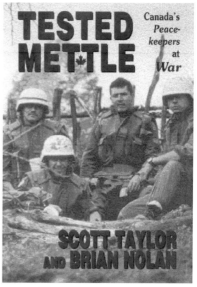

*"Apparently, what distinguishes NATO's killing
and maiming of innocents from Serbian
war crimes is that NATO acts
in the name of humanity."*

**INAT
"Resetting the Stage"**